SCRAMBLES IN LOCHABER

A GUIDE TO SCRAMBLES IN AND AROUND LOCHABER - INCLUDING BEN NEVIS AND GLENCOE

Noel Williams
Illustrations by the author

CICERONE PRESS
MILNTHORPE, CUMBRIA

Frontispiece:
Curved Ridge, Buachaille Etive Mor, Glencoe (Route 47).
Front Cover:
The South face of A'Chailleach, Glencoe, (Route 26).
Not quite as frightening as it appears! The camera angle makes the slab-angle ramp appear much steeper than it is.
Back cover:
Aonach Eagach, Glencoe, (Route 25).

ISBN 0 902363 57 3

First published 1985
Reprinted 1989

CONTENTS

'They (Glencoe and Lochaber) had everything: peak, plateau, precipice, the thinnest of ridges, and green valley, all set between the widest of wild moors and a narrow sea-loch - they were Baghdad and Samarkand, at once home and goal of the pilgrim.'

W.H.Murray, 'Undiscovered Scotland'.

'Nothing is more invigorating and delightful, or better calculated to make one forgetful of little ills, than landing at a picturesque spot for a few hours' scramble on cliffs and rocks.'

R.T.McMullen, 'Down Channel'.

* * *

ACKNOWLEDGEMENTS

When I started working on this guide about eighteen months ago, I did not appreciate quite how limited my knowledge of the area was. More than a decade's climbing in the area had given me a rather restricted view of the local mountains. I hope these scrambles will help others discover some of the delights to be found in the wilder parts of Lochaber.

The phenomenally good weather this spring and summer made my task much easier than it might have been. One memorable day in April, Fort William was the hottest place in Europe. Who says it always rains in Fort William?

Many people have helped me in various ways in the realization of this guide. Ed Grindley first suggested the idea and outlined the Glencoe section. Gordon Rothero also made helpful comments on the Glencoe section. Several local Munroists, notably 'Skoobie' Paterson, Donald Watt and Richard Wood, gave me the benefit of their extensive knowledge of the area. Tim Beesley, Carolyn Hill, Danny McShane, Simon Poulson and various pupils from Lochaber High School accompanied me on some of the scrambles. Alex and Mary Gillespie and Peter MacRae suggested a number of scrambles. To these and any others who helped me in any way, I extend my thanks.

I also acknowledge the help received from the various editions of the Scottish Mountaineering Club district guides. These are mines of information and contain the accumulated experience of several generations of Scottish hillgoers.

Noel Williams, Fort William 1984.

INTRODUCTION

This guide describes some of the best scrambles to be found within 45km radius of the town of Fort William, an area which includes not only Ben Nevis and Glencoe, but also Ben Alder to the east, Ben Cruachan to the south, Garbh Bheinn to the west and The Saddle to the north. Most of this area falls within the Lochaber District of Highland Region. It is the most popular area in the whole of Scotland with hillgoers, and justifiably so, for it contains some of the most varied and spectacular mountain scenery in the Highlands.

Fort William is readily accessible by road and rail and serves as a centre for the tourist and outdoor enthusiast alike. Looming over the town is the highest mountain in the British Isles, Ben Nevis. 'The Ben' attracts the attention of peak-baggers from many nations, but the tourist path to its summit is one of the dullest and most crowded up any mountain in the country. This guide is for those who seek more interesting routes than this.

A number of the scrambles described here have been popular for years and are fairly well worn, but many others are little frequented and consequently have a certain pioneering atmosphere about them. Some experience of route finding will be useful in such cases. The majority of scrambles involve lengthy sections of hillwalking in approach or descent, and this should be taken into account when planning an outing.

What Is Scrambling?

The term scrambling is normally used to describe progress which is too exciting to be just hillwalking, but not difficult enough to be genuine rock climbing. It involves using the hands but not usually a rope. However, it would be wrong to underestimate the serious nature of this form of mountain travel. The terrain may be vegetated, the rock less than perfect, and the consequences of a slip unpleasant to contemplate. **It is worth remembering that unroped scrambling in exposed situations is potentially the most dangerous of all mountaineering activities.**

Although in many cases a rope will not be felt necessary, some knowledge of rock climbing and rope management may be required on the more difficult scrambles. This can be especially true if deteriorating weather conditions necessitate a retreat. A rope in the hands of an experienced hillgoer can also help reassure a novice on a difficult section. One of the attractions of scrambling, however, is being able to move freely, unfettered by the full range of rock climbing equipment.

Grading Of Scrambles

All the scrambles are described and graded for DRY, SUMMER conditions. They would be completely different undertakings in the wet or in winter. It should be remembered that snow and ice persist on the higher mountains well into the summer. Many summer scrambles become serious winter climbs suitable only for experienced mountaineers.

The following grades are used:

Grade 1 relatively straightforward scrambles in which the difficulties are short and usually avoidable. The exposure is unlikely to be great.

Grade 2 rather more demanding scrambles in which the difficulties are less easily avoided. They sometimes contain exposed sections and a rope may occasionally be felt necessary.

Grade 3 more serious scrambles which contain pitches involving easy rock climbing. There may be considerable exposure in places. All but experienced climbers would prefer the reassurance of a rope on some sections. A knowledge of abseiling might prove useful in the event of retreat.

Grade 3(S) indicates scrambles which are particularly serious undertakings perhaps because of continuous exposure, poor rock, vegetation, lack of belays or difficulties of retreat. Short pitches may be up to Moderate rock climbing standard.

In practice it is difficult to apply these grades with any great precision. The line and hence the difficulty of some scrambles can be varied at will. Others have only very short sections of difficulty amidst easy ground. Some hillgoers become very nervous in exposed positions even when the difficulties are not great.

In some cases intermediate grades such as 2/3 have been given. Where there are alternative ways of negotiating a section of a route, this is shown for example as Grade 1 or 2.

Stars are used to indicate the overall quality of the scrambles. The more stars the better the route, although an absence of stars does not mean a route is without merit. Three stars are reserved for outings which are particularly good, because of their continuous interest or fine position.

Maps

The O.S. 1:50,000 Landranger maps are not always adequate for use with this guide. The 1:25,000 Pathfinder maps are preferred and recommended. They give much better contour information and show walls, fences, forest tracks and rides missing on the smaller scale maps.

Six-figure grid references are used in the text to aid the location of some features. These grid references pinpoint a 100m square within which the feature (or most of it) can be found.

Grid references are explained on the margins of 1:50,000 O.S. maps, and an example is given below.

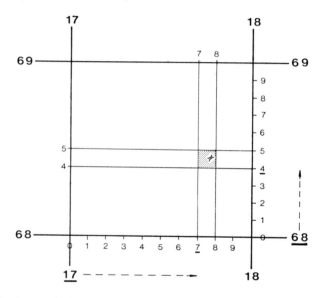

The feature is the wire bridge at Steall, Glen Nevis. Its six-figure grid reference is 177 684 and by using this the reader should be able to find the bridge on Sheet NN 06/16 (1:25,000 Kinlochleven) or on Sheet 41 (1:50,000 Ben Nevis).

Heights And Distances

All heights and distances in this guide are expressed in metres and kilometres. Those unfamiliar with metric units can convert them with reasonable accuracy by using the following -

$$10m = 33 \text{ feet}$$
$$1km = \frac{5}{8} \text{ mile}$$

Since many scrambles have long approaches, the following rules may help those wishing to estimate the time required for the hillwalking part of an outing.

i) **Allow** 12 minutes per km (5 k.p.h.) - good terrain, fit party
or 15 minutes per km (4 k.p.h.) - rough terrain, less fit party.

ii) **Add** 10 minutes per 100m of height gained
i.e. 1 minute per contour on metric maps.

This is a metricated version of 'Naismith's Rule'. It does not include an allowance for stops or rests. Obviously it does not apply to scrambling as such. The grid of 1km squares on O.S. maps can be used for measuring distances quickly.

Navigation

The ability to navigate is the single most important skill required of those who travel in the hills. Fortunately ours is a magnetic planet. Most hillgoers take advantage of this by learning how to use a compass properly in conjunction with a map. Harold Raeburn, doyen of Scottish mountaineers, was a little uncomplimentary to scramblers in an early S.M.C. guide.

'Every mountaineer, of course, carries a compass and
map. Without them he is merely a scrambler.'

ALL hillgoers should know how to use a map and compass. Beginners may not be familiar with one of the most important navigation exercises which involves the following steps:

1. Take a grid bearing off the map by using the compass as a protractor.
2. Convert the grid bearing to a magnetic bearing by allowing for 'grid-magnetic variation'. In Lochaber at present (1984), this means ADDING 6° to the grid bearing, but see the margin of a current map to find out how this varies with time.
3. Set the compass and walk on the magnetic bearing.

This exercise is of paramount importance in conditions of poor visibility, which are only too prevalent in the Highlands.

Those unsure of their navigating ability might find participation in an orienteering event particularly instructive. This sport highlights the fact that estimating distances is an important part of navigation. Distances can be estimated either by timing or by pacing. If timing is used, you have to be able to gauge your speed of travel fairly accurately. This is similar to applying Naismith's rule in reverse. Some people prefer to estimate distances by pacing, but this requires prior knowledge of your own pace length.

To determine your own 'double pace' length, measure out a certain distance, say 100m, and then walk it, counting every time the same foot touches the ground. Most people take between 60 and 70 double paces to cover 100m. Someone taking almost 67 double paces to cover 100m can convert a distance in metres to number of double paces by multiplying by $\frac{2}{3}$.

Such calculations can be critical on some occasions and rather than run the risk of making a mistake when under pressure, some hillwalkers carry Timing/Pacing Charts along with their map in a plastic case. An example is shown below.

DISTANCE IN METRES	TIME (mins and secs)			NUMBER OF DOUBLE PACES		
50	1.00	0.45	0.36	36	33	31
100	2.00	1.30	1.12	71	67	63
200	4.00	3.00	2.24	143	133	125
300	6.00	4.30	3.36	214	200	188
400	8.00	6.00	4.48	286	267	250
500	10.00	7.30	6.00	357	333	313
600	12.00	9.00	7.12	429	400	375
700	14.00	10.30	8.24	500	467	438
800	16.00	12.00	9.36	571	533	500
900	18.00	13.30	10.48	643	600	563
1000	20.00	15.00	12.00	714	667	625
	3 kph	4 kph	kph	1.4m	1.5m	1.6m
		SPEED			DOUBLE PACE LENGTH	

Weather

The weather in the Highlands is likely to be cloudier, colder, wetter, and windier than elsewhere. Indeed, this guide includes an area around Loch Quoich with the highest rainfall in the whole country. Good days are to be relished when they occur. The best months are normally May and June. July and August are warmer but wetter.

11

There is more rainfall in the west than in the east and more on the mountains than on low ground.

Some figures from the former observatory on the summit of Ben Nevis (for the seventeen years 1884-1901) may be of interest.

The mean annual temperature on the summit was just below 0°C. This was almost 9°C lower than the mean annual temperature for Fort William, indicating a fall in temperature of about 1°C for every 150m of height gained. The mean annual rainfall on the summit was 4.00m, more than double that for Fort William in the same period
Winds on the summit were over twice as strong as those at sea level. Some monthly extremes for the summit are listed below;

Wettest	- December
Windiest	- January
Coldest	- February and March
Deepest Snow	- April
Driest	- May and June
Sunniest	- June
Hottest	- July and August

Snow and ice may linger on the summit of Ben Nevis well into the summer. Ice axes and crampons can be put to good use on the mountain later than many suppose. Snow patches often survive in the northern gullies through to the following winter. Consequently some of the scrambles on Ben Nevis do not come into condition until late in the summer. Snow is usually lying on the summit again by the end of October.

Access

During the stalking season, from mid-August until mid-October, there are likely to be restrictions on access to the majority of estates. It is sometimes possible for small parties to obtain permission from the estate factor or stalker to visit parts of an estate where stalking is not taking place on a given day. Otherwise, hillgoers are not welcome at this time. It is vital to the economy of these estates that deer stalking takes place without disruption.

Details of restrictions and the names and addresses of estate contacts can be found in a small booklet entitled 'Access for Mountaineers and Hillwalkers', published by the Mountaineering Council of Scotland and the Scottish Landowners' Federation. There are no restrictions of this kind on Ben Nevis and National Trust for Scotland land at Glencoe and Kintail.

Equipment

Normal hillwalking gear is appropriate for scrambling. This should include waterproofs as well as map and compass. The choice of footwear for scrambling is particularly important. Many mountain accidents over the years have been blamed on a 'simple slip in smooth-soled shoes'.

There is a bewildering variety of boots available nowadays in outdoor shops. Cheap bendy boots, such as fell boots, are not suitable. Rigid mountaineering boots are too clumsy and expensive. The ideal scrambling boot is of medium weight, with a semi-stiff sole and a narrow welt. It should maintain good frictional properties in the wet. The tread pattern, whether vibram-type or klet-type, should be deep enough to grip well on muddy ground. Since the majority of accidents to hillwalkers occur during descent, thought should also be given to the heel design of boots. Smooth or rounded heels can be lethal.

If a rope is to be carried, at least one member of the party needs to be fully conversant with belaying techniques. A few slings, karabiners and a selection of nuts will also prove useful. It goes without saying that such equipment will only give an illusion of safety if it is used incorrectly.

The Italian Hitch, which requires no special equipment apart from an H.M.S karabiner, is a simple and effective method of belaying, especially for bringing up a second. However, it must not be used on hawser laid rope. Devices of the Sticht Plate type are also very effective, reasonably easy to use and light to carry. The classic method of belaying, where the rope is passed around the body and twisted over an arm, is less foolproof than the other two methods, because if the rope is not positioned carefully it may be pulled from the back of the belayer in the event of a fall. Whichever method is used, there should be no slack in the system and the rope should be arranged in such a way that it cannot run over and hence melt through the main belay. Gloves should be worn for belaying, particularly for the classic method.

On the more difficult scrambles, if bad weather deters further progress, a retreat by abseil may sometimes be necessary. It is possible to abseil with just a rope using the classic method, and it is worthwhile being familiar with this method for emergencies. However it is much more comfortable to abseil with a sit sling and one can be made easily from a long tape and a screwgate karabiner. If there is no tree available to double the rope round, a sling may also be required for an anchor.

Small day sacks are very useful for carrying equipment and food. Very large sacks, notably those with external frames, should be avoided since they snag more easily and may unbalance the scrambler.

Accommodation

There are official camp sites in Glen Nevis and Glencoe which provide all main facilities. There is also plenty of scope for free roadside camping, particularly in Glencoe and Glen Etive. Several mountaineering clubs have huts in the area, but these have to be booked in advance through a club secretary. They include Steall Cottage (Lochaber Mountaineering Club) at G.R. 177 683, the C.I.C. Hut (Scottish Mountaineering Club) at G.R. 167 722, Lagangarbh (Scottish Mountaineering Club) at G.R. 220 559, Blackrock Cottage (Ladies' Scottish Climbing Club) at G.R. 267 530, and Inbhir-fhaolain (Grampian Mountaineering Club) at G.R. 158 507.

Youth Hostels are situated in Glen Nevis and Glencoe, by Loch Ossian, Loch Lochy and Loch Duich, and near Crianlarich, Oban and Morar. There are various bunkhouses and self-catering cottages in Glencoe, Glen Nevis, near Torlundy and at Fersit. Bed and breakfast is available in much of the area, and bookings can be made through the tourist office in Fort William. There are also many hotels in the area, such as the Kingshouse Hotel at the western end of Rannoch Moor, and the Clachaig Inn in Glencoe.

Numerous open bothies are dotted throughout the remoter parts of Lochaber, and details of these are available from the Mountain Bothies Association. The buildings are owned by the estates concerned, but members of the M.B.A. help to maintain them on a voluntary basis. It is only sensible fo leave bothies tidy and to take away litter. Some owners have demolished bothies in the past, because of the mess or damage done by visitors.

Geology

A little knowledge of geology can help the outdoor enthusiast to appreciate how the local hills were formed. Numerous features of geological interest occur within the area, some of which are world famous. Many different rocks are exposed in the mountains of Lochaber, and it does not take an expert to notice their different colours, textures and frictional properties.

The rocks of the Highlands represent the eroded root of an ancient mountain chain, called the Caledonian Mountain Chain, which once extended from Greenland and Scandinavia, across Britain to Newfoundland and the eastern side of North America. Continental drift and erosion have subsequently fragmented and worn down this mountain chain, which at one time must have been similar to the present-day Andes.

The Caledonian mountain-building episode, which finished about 400 million years ago, involved marine sediments which had been deposited some 200 million years earlier. As a result of the great heat and pressure exerted on the original sediments, a variety of metamorphic or 'changed' rocks were produced. Mud was changed into slate, silt changed into schist, clean quartz sand changed to quartzite, and limy sediment changed to metamorphic limestone or marble. These rocks were all folded on a gigantic scale and many of them were thrown into 'nappe' structures, which resulted in the rocks becoming completely overturned.

At the end of the same mountain-building episode, a considerable quantity of molten rock material, or magma, was formed in the base of the mountain chain. Some of this erupted to the surface and produced several hundred metres of lava flows, such as those seen in Glencoe and Ben Nevis. The remainder cooled within the earth's crust to produce great masses of granite and countless NE-SW trending dykes. A process called 'cauldron-subsidence' complicated the situation in Glen Etive, Glencoe and Ben Nevis. In these localities the roof above a chamber of magma fractured in such a way that a cylindrical plug of rock was formed, which then sank into the magma before it crystallised. The lavas in Glencoe and Ben Nevis would have been eroded away many years ago, had they not subsided hundreds of metres in this manner.

The Great Glen Fault, was most active shortly after this igneous activity. Movement along the fault resulted in the whole of north-west Scotland sliding some considerable distance horizontally, relative to the rest of the country. The rocks along the fault were crushed and shattered by the movement and consequently were eroded more easily to form the Great Glen. The fault has remained a line of weakness to the present day and there are still occasional tremors along it.

For more than 300 million years processes of erosion wore down the Caledonian Mountains. During this time the British area gradually drifted northwards from the southern hemisphere, crossing the equator some 300 million years ago. Then, about 60 million years ago when the North Atlantic was opening, further igneous activity occurred down the west coast of Scotland. Many NW-SE trending dykes in Lochaber date from this time.

Within the last 500,000 years ice sheets and glaciers have advanced and retreated over Scotland many times, carving out the familiar landforms we see today. The earth's crust was depressed by the great weight of ice that covered it, but now that the ice has gone it is bouncing back up again. This is happening at a rate of over 3 mm/year in the region of Rannoch Moor - Munro-baggers please note! However, it would only need a slight change in climate for the ice to return, since the summit of Ben Nevis is just a few hundred metres below the present level of permanent snows for this latitude.

History

No guide to the hills of Lochaber would be complete without a mention of the wanderings of Prince Charles Edward Stuart after his defeat at Culloden in April 1746. He traversed the district several times that summer, often drenched to the skin, plagued by midges and in constant fear of his life, before escaping to France in September of the same year. Those who trace his steps in the area today can only admire his hardiness and marvel at the loyalty of his followers.

By the time the clan system ended in 1775, tens of thousands of Highlanders had emigrated to North America. Over the next hundred years, thousands more were forcibly evicted from their homes and shipped abroad to make way for sheep. Many boats packed with emigrants sailed from Fort William during this period.

At the same time, communications in the Highlands gradually improved. In the early part of the nineteenth century Thomas Telford was responsible for cutting the Caledonian Canal through the Great Glen, but more importantly he also constructed new roads and bridges, and rebuilt some of the old military roads.

Last, but not least, the completion of the railway to Fort William in 1894 opened up the region still further. Several scrambles described in this guide were first ascended by parties who travelled north by train in the years immediately after the opening of the West Highland Line.

Fauna and Flora

Many different animals and plants will be encountered by hillgoers in Lochaber. Only the obvious ones are mentioned here. Red deer are plentiful and although usually seen only at a distance, great herds of them occur throughout the area. Ptarmigan are numerous on high ground, but their camouflage is normally so good that they go unnoticed. They are reluctant fliers and if disturbed will walk away rapidly, the hens frantically dragging a wing to distract from their chicks.

Unfortunately, certain other creatures make their presence felt more forcefully in the summer months. These are the blood-sucking midges, clegs and sheep-ticks. Although clegs have very painful bites, and sheep-ticks produce unpleasant, itchy sores where they burrow in the skin, it is the midges which are the most troublesome overall, because of their countless numbers. They can be unbearable at dawn and dusk, and after rain on windless days. Repellants are a must for those wishing to camp in poorly drained glens.

It will be noticed that the vegetation on our hills changes gradually with increasing altitude. Heather and peat-bog give way to bilberry and crowberry heaths and to grass heaths. Arctic, alpine and arctic-alpine plants make up the mountain flora. Late in the summer, ripe bilberries provide pleasant fare on several scrambles in the area.

The remains of tree stumps, exposed in peat-bogs, tell of a drier climate in the recent past. Tree-felling by man completed the devastation of the ancient woodlands. Grazing by sheep and deer is preventing natural regeneration. Lochaber was once famous for its oakwoods, but regimented conifers have now taken over.

*   *   *

The scrambles are arranged into four groups:
1. East of Fort William
2. South of Fort William
3. West of Fort William
4. North of Fort William

The first two areas are separated from the last two by the Great Glen.

Castle Ridge and the Castle, Ben Nevis (Route 6)

THE EASTERN
GROUP

The Ben Nevis Range

The magnificent Ben Nevis Range, which extends some 15km eastwards from Fort William, is one of the finest groups of mountains in the land. It receives most attention at its western end, where the mighty Ben Nevis is readily accessible from Glen Nevis. The remainder of the range, though less lofty, is remarkably varied, and being in a wilder setting provides a delightful contrast to the major peak.

Ben Nevis itself has a Jekyll and Hyde character, appearing a dull hump from the west and a fiercesome precipice from the north-east. Those approaching it for the first time along the Allt a' Mhuilinn cannot fail to be impressed by the grandeur of its north-east face.

*   *   *

MEALL AN T-SUIDHE   *(Hill of the seat)*

The first part of the tourist path up Ben Nevis skirts around Meall an t-Suidhe (pronounced 'Melantee'), but very few of those who ascend Ben Nevis this way make a detour to its top. Both the scrambles described here are suitable for a short day or an evening, and they can often be done when weather conditions rule out the higher peaks. They are very convenient for those staying in Glen Nevis. There is a fine panorama from the summit which takes in Lochan Meall an t-Suidhe (commonly called the 'halfway lochan') on one side, and Loch Eil and the Great Glen on the other. Since the busy tourist path passes directly below these scrambles the greatest care should be taken not to dislodge any stones or rocks.

On the south-western aspect of Meall an t-Suidhe, directly across from the Youth Hostel in Glen Nevis, there are three parallel buttresses. To the left of these is a broad, grassy gully called Slochd an Daimh *(gully of the stag)*. The lefthand buttress is broader and more broken than the other two on which the scrambles are now described.

1. CENTRAL SOUTH-WEST BUTTRESS   Grade 2

This scramble is probably more enjoyable early or late in the season when bracken is not established on the lower slopes. The upper half consists of a heathery, broken granite ridge. The granite is rather

MEALL AN T-SUIDHE

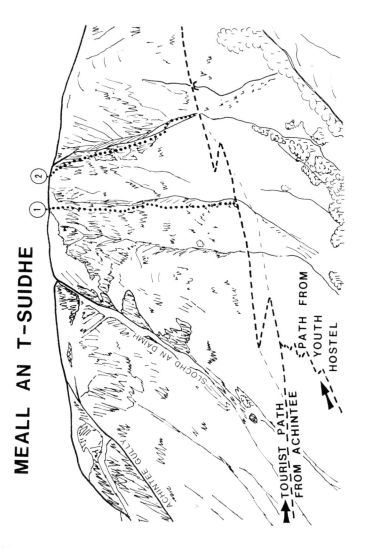

ACHINTEE GULLY

SLOCHD AN DAIMH

TOURIST PATH FROM ACHINTEE

PATH FROM YOUTH HOSTEL

lichenous and the route is not recommended in the wet.

Reach Achintee either along the single-track road from Claggan, or via a footbridge over the River Nevis from the picnic area in Glen Nevis. (Achintee is a corruption of Achadh an t-Suidhe, meaning *'field of the seat')*. Follow the tourist path for 1km to its junction with the path from the Youth Hostel. This provides a shorter but steeper alternative start. Continue through a zig-zag in the path and cross a prominent stream. 100 metres further on, a tiny rock buttress abuts against the path. Immediately to the right of this is another stream.

Scramble up the front of the buttress to easier ground. By moving to and fro, several further sections of slabby rock can be incorporated, before a long grassy slope is reached. The main part of the scramble begins at the top of this.

Ascend step-like rocks . overlooking the gully on the right. Continue up the heathery ridge, weaving to and fro over rounded granite blocks. Careful route finding is required in places and the easiest line is not always apparent. There are some loose blocks in places, but these are usually obvious. The angle eventually eases, and the route finishes on the 682m top. The summit of Meall an t-Suidhe is 500m to the north across a shallow col. Running south-west from this col is a broad grassy gully, boulder-strewn in places. This is the Sloch an Daimh, and it gives a quick line of descent to the tourist path.

2. RIGHT-HAND SOUTH-WEST BUTTRESS   Grade 1   *
Approach as for the previous route and follow the tourist path through the second zig-zag. Reach a prominent stream some 50m short of the first Aluminium Bridge. Ascend the bed of the stream easily at first. Then bridge up the gully where it narrows. There are several short steep sections before the gully widens out and the angle eases. If there is too much water in the stream or if the bridging proves too difficult, it is possible to scramble easily up the grassy slope left of the gully.

Where the gully broadens, move out left onto the buttress. This is followed all the way up the hillside until it peters out. The scrambling is on rough heathery granite. Any difficulties can easily be avoided if necessary. Descend as for the previous route.

*   *   *

Ben Nevis viewed from the S.W.

BEN NEVIS

The summit of Ben Nevis and its north-west top, Carn Dearg, together form an extensive pincer-like plateau which encloses the complex north-east face of the mountain. A spur running down off the flank of this plateau leads to the south-west top, which is also called Carn Dearg *(red stony rounded summit)*. This spur separates two large corries to the south and to the west of the summit. The southern one is called Coire Eoghainn *(Ewen's Corrie)*, and the western one is called Coire Ghaimhnean *(Corrie of skins?)*, although this is more commonly known as Five Finger Gully. A narrow curving ridge links Ben Nevis to Carn Mor Dearg, and this is called the Carn Mor Dearg Arête, or simply 'The Arête'.

The tourist path ascends the broad west-north-west shoulder of the mountain by a series of large zig-zags. These are confined to the north by 'The Red Burn' and to the south by Five Finger Gully. The path straightens out as it reaches the plateau and passes close to the top of Tower Gully before turning sharply at the top of Gardyloo Gully. A small emergency shelter is perched on the ruins of the Observatory close by the summit trig point.

Ben Nevis is world famous for its winter climbing and the mountain holds snow for much of the year. This means that some of the scrambles may be possible as such for only two months in the summer, and even the tourist path holds snow surprisingly late. Descent from the summit requires care in bad visibility, especially if there is still snow on the plateau. Many parties, anxious to avoid the north-east face, have strayed too far the other way, and ended up in Coire Eoghainn or Five Finger Gully.

From the summit trig point it is important first to reach the corner at the top of Gardyloo Gully. This is 150m away (100 double paces?) on a grid bearing of 231° (237° magnetic in 1984). Once past this indent a grid bearing of 281° (287° magnetic in 1984) leads safely off the mountain to the middle of the main zig-zags on the tourist path.

The first three scrambles all start from Glen Nevis and are less serious outings. All the other scrambles are on the north-east face, and are approached along the glen of the Allt a' Mhuilinn *(stream of the mill)*.

3. SURGEON'S RIB   Grade 1 or 3

The western flank of Ben Nevis is seamed by several major gullies. One of these gullies is easy to identify, because a prominent stone wall runs straight up to it from the floor of Glen Nevis. It is marked on the 1:10,000 O.S. map as Allt an Aon Doruis *(stream of the single gash)*, but for many years it has been known as Surgeon's Gully after the local surgeon who pioneered a climb up it. The scramble now described follows a line on the north side of this gully.

The approach used for this scramble depends on the intended descent route. For those descending by the tourist path from Ben Nevis, the best starting place is the footbridge at the Youth Hostel. For those descending southwards to Polldudh, the car park at the Lower Falls (G.R. 145 684) is more convenient. Either approach involves a walk of about 2km along the east bank of the River Nevis. In very dry conditions it is possible to wade across the river near the Old Grave Yard at G.R. 136 701.

Go easily up the hillside to the top of the dry stone wall. Continue up the north bank of Surgeon's Gully, following sheep tracks where possible. This can be made more interesting by staying close to the gully and peering in at the waterfalls from time to time.

The way ahead is eventually barred by a broken rock band which, if taken direct, gives the major difficulties of the day. An easier

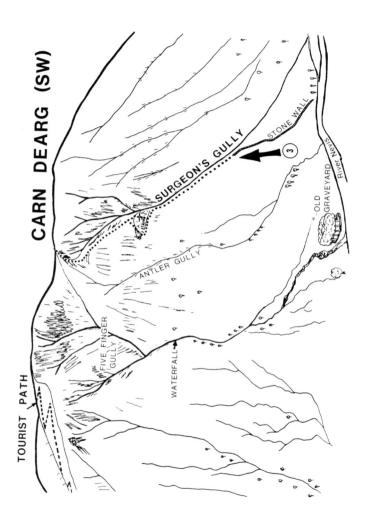

CARN DEARG (SW)

SURGEON'S GULLY

STONE WALL

③

River Nevis

OLD GRAVEYARD

ANTLER GULLY

FIVE FINGER GULLY

WATERFALL

TOURIST PATH

route, more in keeping with the general standard of the outing, traverses a long way left at this point and then takes a faint gully back right to the crest of the buttress, (Grade 1).

The more direct line involves steep scrambling on heathery granite, (Grade 3). Move left from the edge of the gully to the base of the rock band. Zig-zag up the centre of this on heathery ledges, then trend right as far as possible to an awkward groove. Step across this with difficulty and move up to a large grass terrace. The second part of the rock bank looks easy, but in fact it is deceptively steep. Ascend steep heather at first and then traverse right until a series of rough granite slabs are reached. Weave a way up these to easier ground. The rock is excellent, but the easiest line is rather devious.

The going now becomes little more than walking, but the views are good. This side of the mountain is little frequented and deer can sometimes be seen here. Where Surgeon's Gully splits into three branches, a well-worn deer track contours the hillside.

At one point higher up, a rock step is reached which has a large flake of rock precariously perched on it. Pass this on the right. Another easy section then leads to some pleasant scrambling up a series of rock steps, before a flattening on the ridge is reached. From here the final section of ridge can be seen curving up to the right. Several interesting little outcrops can be sought out at the bottom of this ridge. Higher up it becomes narrower but more bouldery. It then levels out and merges into the broad ridge connecting Carn Dearg (SW) to the main mass of Ben Nevis. The summit of Carn Dearg (1020m) is about 400m to the south.

There are various options from here. The south-west shoulder of Ben Nevis can be followed until the tourist path is reached at a height of about 1250m. From the summit of Carn Dearg it is possible to head east and eventually descend by the waterslide to the car park at the head of Glen Nevis. A more interesting descent from Carn Dearg can be made down the shoulder separating the southern and western flanks of the top. The way is obvious at first, but lower down it is best to move off the crest into a grassy runnel on the left. Eventually an undulating col is reached which leads to the top above the Polldubh Crags, called Am Mam Buidhe *(the yellow hill)*. Devotees of these crags will be able to descend fairly directly from here. Otherwise follow the western ridge and near the bottom of this turn south to the sheep fank by the Lower Falls.

* * *

Glen Nevis - Scimitar Ridge in the foreground (Route 4)
Meall Cumhann behind (Route 5)

MAM BEAG, POLLDUBH

On the north side of the Glen Nevis road, where it becomes single track just after the Lower Falls, the hillside is littered for more than 1km with numerous rock outcrops. These are the Polldubh Crags and they provide many delightful short rock climbs at all grades of difficulty. The rock is mica schist but it is less friable here than elsewhere, because it was 'baked' (thermally metamorphosed) by heat from the neighbouring granite intrusions.

The scramble now described takes a ridge running along the top of a crag known to climbers as Scimitar Buttress. It is so called because of a curious scimitar-shaped boulder on the slope nearby. On the O.S. 1:25,000 map the summit is marked as Mam Beag, 212m *(small hill)*. The scramble starts near to the road and although short, it gives a pleasant introduction to the Polldubh Crags as well as some fine views of the glen. It can be done in the wet.

4. SCIMITAR RIDGE Grade 1/2

This route follows the south-west ridge of Mam Beag which is easily seen when travelling east along the road from the Lower Falls. Park at a large passing place either at G.R. 154 684 or at G.R. 156 684, and walk up to the col behind the first bump on the ridge.

Go up to the first rock band and start at a vague groove in the centre. Move up to an obvious foot ledge, then step left. Pull up on a good hold to a broad slab. Traverse left along a narrow grassy ledge and go easily up a crack to a grassy recess. Ascend the rib on the left of this using a good flake handhold. Continue more easily, staying as close as possible to the crest of the ridge.

Move up the next big rock step, left of centre, then step right and ascend by a prominent quartz vein. Continue easily to a huge boulder slab. Scramble delightfully up this and reach a grassy runnel running up from the left. Go directly leftwards across this back to the ridge crest. There is a steep drop on the left at this point. Reach a short rock step with a crack on the left. Go up the right side of this and continue easily to the flat summit of Mam Beag.

From here there are fine views of the crags at the east end of Polldubh. Slabs Wall is prominent and this provides several easier grade rock climbs which are suitable for beginners. Details of these and a host of other rock routes in the area can be found in 'Glen Nevis and the Lochaber Outcrops' by Ed Grindley *(Cicerone Press)*.

To descend, pass over the summit, drop down to the north and turn left. Walk easily down the grassy slope parallel to the line of ascent, passing the scimitar-like boulder en route.

* * *

It is possible to find some scrambling on the southern slope of Carn Dearg above Polldubh, but it is generally very disappointing. The last scramble described from this side of Ben Nevis is on Meall Cumhann and this is reached through the Glen Nevis Gorge.

*   *   *

MEALL CUMHANN

Tagged on to the south-east shoulder of Ben Nevis is a top called Meall Cumhann *(hill of the gorge)*. Despite its modest stature (698m), it is one of the most delightful hills hereabouts, and gives magnificent views of Glen Nevis, Coire Guibhsachan and The Mamores. From the car park at the end of Glen Nevis, a popular walk leads through the spectacular Nevis gorge to a flat meadow with

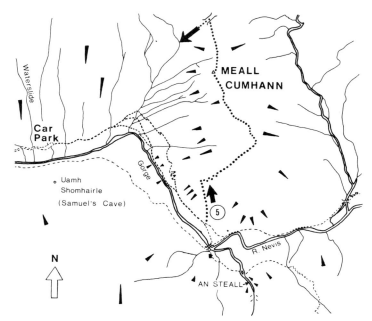

fine views of An Steall *(the cataract).* Not many people realise that there are paths at three different levels on this side of the river as well as another on the western side.

The best known path is the middle path. The lower path leaves this shortly after a gangway cut in red granite across a stream, and then rejoins it at a broad gully filled with huge boulders from a recent rock-fall. The upper path leaves the middle path about 100m after the lower one and then gradually gains height before zig-zagging down to rejoin it just after the gorge.

5. THE TRAVERSE OF MEALL CUMHANN   Grade 1   *

Follow any of these paths to the meadow just after the gorge. Continue towards An Steall and reach a fork in the path about 150m short of the wire bridge leading to Steall Cottage. Turn back left and slant northwards up the grassy hillside to a tiny col above a crag known as Meadow Crag. This col can also be approached from the other side, but it is not so easy to identify from that direction.

Head up the broad broken ridge picking out small rock outcrops to

28

add interest. Eventually emerge on a pleasant section of whaleback slab. Go up this to the crest of the hill and then turn left towards the summit. A series of rock bands run across the ridge and these give scrambling to suit all tastes. Generally the easiest lines are to be found on the right. The views are superb.

From the summit continue easily down the north ridge. At one point some tottering pinnacles can be seen just below the ridge on the Glen Nevis side. Reach Bealach Cumhann, and then head south-west across the hillside back to the car park.

*   *   *

THE NORTH-EAST FACE OF BEN NEVIS

It would be difficult to exaggerate the grandeur of this face of the mountain. For more than 2km a complex sequence of ridges, gullies, walls and buttresses soars up from the floor of the Glen of the Allt a' Mhuilinn. Rarely is this side of the mountain completely free of snow. The scrambles all have a serious air about them, and newcomers are advised to try the easier ones first to familiarise themselves with the scale and layout of the mountain.

There are four possible approaches to the face:

i)   Park at the golf course 3km out of Fort William on the A82 Inverness Road. Cross the golf course and go over a stile at a deep drainage ditch. Continue up the hillside through a boggy section to a second stile. Carry on up, quite steeply for some distance, until the angle eases at a large yellow crane by a dam on the Allt a' Mhuilinn. This is an intake point for the British Alcan hydro-electric scheme. Follow a boggy path on the east side of the stream all the way to the C.I.C. Hut.

ii) Park about 2 km N.E. of Fort William at some warehouses, 250m after the A830 Mallaig Road turn-off. A path starts from the north side of the Distillery and follows the south bank of the Allt a' Mhuilinn. Go under a railway bridge and after 1km reach the course of a former railway (now removed). There are two options here. Either, turn right and after a short distance join a prominent land-rover track which zig-zags up the hillside, then turn left at a junction and head NE to the dam on the Allt a' Mhuilinn. Or, turn left, cross a stream and then follow a path which slants up the hillside to the same track just before the dam. Take the path on the east side of the Allt a' Mhuilinn as for the first approach.

A	Carn Mor Dearg Arête	H	The Douglas Boulder
B	North-East Buttress	I	Tower Ridge
C	Orion Face	J	The Great Tower
D	Observatory Ridge	K	Garadh na Ciste
E	Observatory Buttress	L	C.I.C. Hut
F	Summit of Ben Nevis	2	Number 2 Gully
G	Gardyloo Gully	M	The Comb

iii) Start in Glen Nevis from Achintee or the Youth Hostel and follow the tourist path to Lochan Meall an t-Suidhe. Then instead of turning south to the Red Burn, follow a path across the plateau to a point overlooking the Allt a' Mhuilinn. Turn right and after losing some height initially, follow a path up to the C.I.C. Hut. This is not quite as boggy as the first two approaches.

iv) From the car park at the head of Glen Nevis follow a path up the east side of the waterslide. Turn right at the top of this and ascend a shoulder leading directly to the Carn Mor Dearg Arête. Descend by some abseil posts into Coire Leis *(leeward corrie)*. This is a very steep approach, probably only of interest to those staying in Steall Cottage.

THE NORTH-EAST FACE OF BEN NEVIS

N	Coire na Ciste	**P**	The Great Buttress of Carn Dearg
3	Number 3 Gully		
4	Number 4 Gully	**Q**	Raeburn's Buttress
O	The Trident Buttresses	**R**	The Castle
5	Number 5 Gully	**S**	Castle Ridge

The scrambles will now be described from right to left, the order in which they appear when approaching up the Allt a' Mhuilinn. They are all on volcanic rocks, comprised of andesite lava flows interspersed with agglomerate. The first major feature on the north-east face is the North Wall of Castle Ridge. This huge triangular wall tends to be dwarfed by the rest of the face, and it receives less attention than it would in humbler surroundings. As early as 1907 Harold Raeburn made a solo ascent of it. Slanting grassy ledges alternate with steep rocky buttresses and some indefinite scrambles can be made. However, the best scrambling hereabouts is on the left-bounding edge of the wall - this is called Castle Ridge. It is one of the major Nevis ridges and the only one which is easy enough to be called a scramble. It gives a superb outing - one of the best in this guide.

6. CASTLE RIDGE   Grade 3(S)   ***

The ridge looks very steep when seen in profile from the Allt a'
Mhuilinn and those not acquainted with it often imagine it to be a
formidable rock climb. In practice, apart from a few steep sections,
it is surprisingly easy-angled. Good route-finding is particularly
important if the easiest line is to be followed. Some rock climbing
experience would be an advantage for the steep crucial section. It is
normally clear of snow relatively early in the season.

Start at the lowest tongue of rock directly above a huge boulder,
known as 'The Lunching Stone', on the path from Lochan Meall an
t-Suidhe. There is a waterfall in a narrow gully about 20m to the left.
Slant up rightwards on slabby rocks, then move left. Keep zig-
zagging up from here. Whenever any difficulties are encountered, a
step left usually allows an easier way to be found. Very sound slabby
rock alternates with grassy steps. Good route-finding pays dividends.
Eventually the angle eases and the terrain becomes grassier.

Now traverse some distance left along a grassy ledge until a steep
move allows access to a broken groove. Ascend this until it is possible
to look into the gully on the left. The ridge can now be seen more
clearly. There are many crampon scratches on the rock from here on.

An alternative start, which traverses from near the C.I.C. Hut all
the way across above a large rock band, joins the ridge at this point.
There are good views across the Castle Corrie on the left, and higher
up, The Castle itself can be seen. This is a wedge-shaped rock
buttress, bounded on the right and left by North Castle Gully and
South Castle Gully respectively.

Head up rightwards on the slabby ridge by any one of a variety of
lines. A short wall is turned on the right by a grassy ledge and a
leftward slanting groove. Higher up, a section of loose boulders is
encountered, but these are not a problem. Eventually the steep
crucial section is reached. Unlike many other parts of the ridge, this
cannot be avoided, (except by a leftwards traverse into North Castle
Gully, but this leads off the ridge completely).

Start up an awkward little corner and then step right. Move across
and up to a steep nose split by a broad crack - this is the crux. It is
exposed and a recent rock-fall has left a scar. On the hardest part the
best holds are not obvious, and it remains steep for about 7m before
a good ledge is reached. A little further on, a steep chimney gives the
last of the difficulties. It is only 3m high and it is soon ascended by
bridging and thrutching.

Continue more easily to a short section of arête. Ascend this and then romp along the crest of the ridge, in one place crossing a massive, flat slab of rock. Emerge on the shoulder of Carn Dearg, overlooking Lochan Meall an t-Suidhe.

Those not wishing to continue over the summit of Carn Dearg can descend the scree-covered slopes directly to Lochan Meall an t-Suidhe. Incidentally, it is curious that Carn Dearg *(red stony summit)* is so-called, because it consists mainly of dark grey-coloured rock.

Due west of the C.I.C. Hut there is a huge rock face comprised of steep ovelapping slabs split by cracks and chimneys. This is the Great Buttress of Carn Dearg. Immediately left of it is a major gully called Number 5 Gully. The next scramble starts up this gully, and then moves out right onto the crest of the buttress and continues up the ridge above to the plateau. It is a splendid route with magnificent views once the ridge has been gained. It is undoubtedly one of the best easy grade scrambles in the area.

7. LEDGE ROUTE   Grade 1   ***

A considerable quantity of snow accumulates in Number 5 Gully over the winter months and consequently the first section of the route can be problematical until the middle of the summer. Any remaining snow should be clearly visible from the C.I.C. Hut.

Start just down from the C.I.C. Hut and scramble delightfully up an apron of rock slabs leading to The Great Buttress. The rock is agglomerate and huge fragments can be seen in it. It was formed from material thrown into the air from a volcano.

When the angle eases, instead of struggling up the scree on the left, head across to the foot of the buttress and then slant up round to the left to the mouth of Number 5 Gully. If there is snow here, it is possible to ascend slabby rocks on the right-hand side of the gully. The easiest line can be difficult to find and is at least Grade 2 standard. Otherwise follow the bed of the gully for some distance until a conspicuous ramp is reached which slants back across the right wall. Follow this easily at first to a short slabby step. Negotiate this, then continue round in a more exposed position to where some water trickles down over broken rocks. Cross this section and then at the first opportunity head up a depression on the left. Continue all the way to the top of this until it is possible to look down a huge sloping shelf into Number 5 Gully.

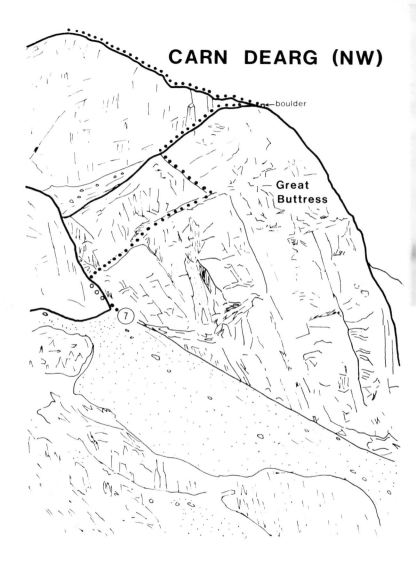

CARN DEARG (NW)

boulder

Great
Buttress

⑦

Ledge Route, Carn Dearg N.W., Ben Nevis (Route 7)

Now turn right and follow the shelf up to a prominent pedestal of shattered rock. Go round a corner on the right to a large platform on the crest of the buttress, with a large boulder on it. There are superb views from here.

Turn left and scramble along the ridge easily at first. The ridge then starts to wind round to the left and as it does so it narrows into a wall for a short section. Either balance along the top of this wall or take an easier option on the right. There are steep drops on the left at this point.

Continue pleasantly along the bouldery ridge for some distance until a flatter section is reached. After this the ridge steepens up again before finishing abruptly on the summit plateau. The true summit of Carn Dearg (1221m) is 300m away around the top of Number 5 Gully. It is easy to descend from here to the tourist path by heading SW across the top of the Red Burn.

Left of Number 5 Gully and forming the right-hand side of Coire na Ciste *(corrie of the chest or coffin)* is a complex rock-mass known as The Trident because of its three main ridges. To the left of this and tucked away in the corner of Coire na Ciste, is Number 4 Gully. This gully descends from the lowest point on the plateau rim, but it cannot be seen from the C.I.C. Hut.

The next scramble takes a direct line up the rocks and vegetation to the right of this gully. It will only be free of snow late in the season.

8.NUMBER FOUR GULLY BUTTRESS   Grade 3

Find a way up the slabby rocks forming the lip of Coire na Ciste. Head up past two small lochans and ascend steep scree to the mouth of Number 4 Gully. A grassy ledge system runs out across the buttress on the right. Start just above this in a chimney/groove which is parallel to the narrow part of Number 4 Gully, but is separated from it by some slabs and a rock rib.

The first few moves bridging up the groove are the hardest on the route. Part way up it is possible to move onto the left (or right) bounding rib. When the groove finishes, continue upwards in the same line. The going becomes easier and rather grassy, but with occasional interest.

Reach a recess with a mossy back wall. Ascend the right wall of this on good holds until able to pull over the top. Slant up easily and emerge near the top of Number 4 Gully by a short square-cut rock wall. Descend by traversing SW to the tourist path, or return to Coire na Ciste down the loose scree in Number 4 Gully.

Number 3 Gully is the most obvious gully at the back of Coire na Ciste when looking SW from the C.I.C. Hut. Between this and Number 4 Gully is a broad buttress called Creag Coire na Ciste. The next route starts up the middle of this buttress and then follows a slanting line to the right.

9. CENTRAL-NORTH ROUTE   Grade 2   *

Snow may be slow to clear from the top part of this route. Although rather devious it gives an enjoyable outing.

Reach the twin lochans in Coire na Ciste as for the previous route, then go up to the lowest tongue of rock in the middle of the crag. Gain this from the left and continue more easily for some distance. Before the rocks start to steepen, cross slabs leftwards and reach a prominent corner with a smooth right wall. Avoid this by easier rocks on the left. When the angle starts to steepen again, head rightwards to a rock nose. Get onto this using big foot ledges on the left, and then make an awkward step up to reach easier rocks.

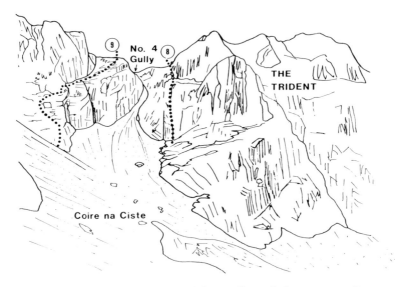

Continue up, slanting slightly right, until an obvious traverse line can be followed on the right. Go rightwards for some distance on an easy ledge. (Hares can sometimes be seen here.) Reach some scree where a gully (North Gully) runs down to the right. Cross this and move out right again to slightly mossy slabs. Ascend these to finish suddenly by the top of Number 4 Gully. Descend as for the previous route.

Some distance to the left of Number 3 Gully a triangular rock buttress, called The Comb, projects into Coire na Ciste. Bounding this on the left is a narrow twisting gully - Comb Gully. Immediately left of this again is another more prominent gully called Number 2 Gully. The following scramble starts at the base of these two gullies and wanders up the face to their left on broken rocks and ledges. It is only advisable late in the season and even then it is liable to be wet in places.

10. RAEBURN'S EASY ROUTE   Grade 2/3

From the C.I.C. Hut, go across to a gorge on the left-hand side of the rock apron guarding Coire na Ciste. Scramble up the right-hand side of a tiny stream which flows down the rocks immediately right of the gorge entrance. Cross over left, and go up slabs and grass for some distance. Stay near to the edge of the gorge, and pass a small rock band to reach a scree slope below a large buttress on the side of Tower Ridge. The summit of this buttress is known as Garadh na Ciste *(garden of the chest or coffin)*, because of its resemblance to a 'Jardin' in the Alps. Continue up steep scree to the bottom of Number 2 Gully.

Slog up the rather unpleasant scree chute emanating from the gully. Reach a mossy rock band which extends some distance to the left. Stay below this and traverse out to its left-hand end. Ascend more broken rock-steps trending left. Reach some scree-covered ledges and go straight up to the next band of clean rock. Make a somewhat awkward move to get started on this, then go up faint parallel grooves on good holds, trending slightly right.

Cross some moss-covered stones to below a large, extensive rock wall. Move up left and join a ledge system leading left. Ascend big, wet rock-steps and break out onto scree to the left of the large wall.

Now slant a long way to the right, above the wall, on a broad terrace covered with scree and moss. Eventually this narrows and steepens slightly as it nears the rim of the plateau. Move carefully up rather slippery mossy slabs on the right side of a mossy gully. Reach the crest on the right and follow this more easily to the plateau. Those with nailed boots (!) may prefer to ascend the mossy gully instead. Join the tourist path, which is close at hand, at a height of 1300m.

Due south of the C.I.C. Hut is the base of the biggest ridge on Ben Nevis - the magnificent Tower Ridge. The bottom part of it consists of a sprawling conical rock buttress called the Douglas Boulder. An ascent of the entire ridge is, unfortunately, just a little bit too hard to be regarded as a scramble. It can be thoroughly recommended to those with climbing experience and it should serve as a goal for ambitious scramblers. Observatory Ridge, on the opposite side of the Observatory Gully on the left, also falls into the same category. Details of these, and many other climbs in the area, can be found in 'Rock and Ice Climbs in Lochaber and Badenoch' by A.C. Stead and J.R.Marshall; 'Climbers' Guide to Ben Nevis' by J.R. Marshall, both published by the Scottish Mountaineering Club, and 'Winter Climbs, Ben Nevis and Glencoe' by Ed Grindley *(Cicerone Press)*.

The scramble now described takes in the middle section of Tower Ridge and then traverses off into Tower Gully near the top. It is a rather contrived line, but very enjoyable nevertheless. It embraces a

38

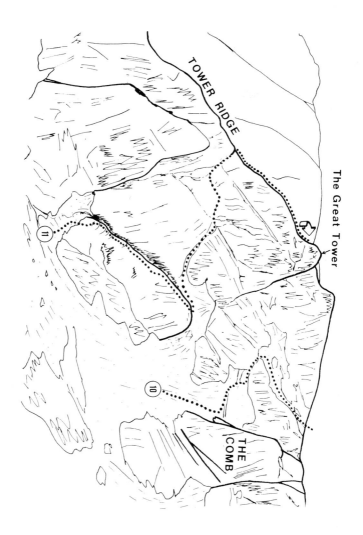

TOWER RIDGE

The Great Tower

THE COMB

variety of situations and has a real mountaineering atmosphere. Tower Gully is one of the highest gullies on Ben Nevis so it will not be free of snow until late in the season.

11. THE CROSSING OF TOWER RIDGE Grade 3(S) **

The route starts by ascending the delightful north-east ridge of Garadh na Ciste on the right-hand flank of Tower Ridge. Reach the base of this as for the previous route.

Move left along an easy ledge to a basin where water issues from the bottom of Garadh Gully. Ascend a wall to the right of this, zig-zagging slightly at first, until an increasingly delicate traverse leads left to the crest overlooking the gully. Go up to easier ground. Continue up grassy grooves and easy rocks to the next steepening. Zig-zag up this section to reach grassier terrain. At the third steepening, trend rightwards to more reasonably angled rock and ascend on good holds to the Garadh na Ciste. There are superb views from this flat stony summit. It is a good place for second thoughts, because it is possible to descend from here to the floor of Coire na Ciste.

Now look back leftwards to where a broken gully (Broad Gully) slants up across the face. Walk across scree to the start of this and ascend it easily at first. When it steepens find a way up a rock rib left of centre.

Emerge at a broken terrace. Keep heading in the same direction along a grassy ledge, which slants gently up to a small shoulder. (Do not go up steep grassy grooves on the right.) Descend the other side of the shoulder on a continuation of the grassy ledge.

At the lowest point, make a rather difficult move to gain a broad grassy gully which rises to the crest of Tower Ridge. Either, go up the gully directly to a small gap on the ridge, or, part way up transfer to rocks on the left instead.

Turn right and go along the ridge to the start of the Little Tower. This is not a tower in fact, but merely a steepening on the ridge. It gives sustained scrambling at a high standard, and constitutes the crux of the route. The rock is excellent and all the holds are well marked with crampon scratches. Variations are possible, but the best line is up huge flakes on the crest.

Ascend another steep section by slanting up to the right and then back left. Reach a flatter part of the ridge at the top of the Little Tower. The major difficulties are now over.

Continue some distance to the base of the Great Tower which gives the ridge its name. Some short sections of scrambling lead to a steep nose. A narrow path, called the Eastern Traverse, goes leftwards round the corner from here. Follow it easily all the way round to a narrow rift capped by a boulder. Ignore this and instead go left to a gap between a gigantic block and the main face. Go down here a few metres to an easy scree-covered ledge. Walk along this and leave the ridge completely.

Reach the base of Tower Gully and clamber up it on very loose scree to the plateau. The tourist path goes past the rim of the gully. Turn left and in less than 300m reach the summit trig point.

CARN MOR DEARG

Ben Nevis is linked by the graceful, curving Carn Mor Dearg Arête to a mountain of remarkably different character. Carn Mor Dearg *(big, red stony summit)* is a granite giant of altogether simpler structure. The next route follows a long pinnacled ridge which leads from the Allt Daim to the summit of Carn Dearg Meadhonach *(middle red stony summit),* a prominent top 500m north-north-west of the main summit. It involves a long approach for only a short section of scrambling, but it gives an excuse to visit a beautifully desolate glen and on a good day there are spectacular views of the Ben Nevis cliffs from the summit.

12. EAST RIDGE OF CARN DEARG MEADHONACH
Grade 1

Park at the golf course 3km NE of Fort William. Cross the golf course (as for the north-east face of Ben Nevis), then instead of going up the hillside, turn left and walk along the course of a former railway (the 'Puggy Line') for 1km to a ride 300m inside a forest. Go up the ride for 150m, turn left at a track and follow this to a T-junction. Turn right and leave the track, after ascending for 250m, at an adit. Head east-south-east to a stream. Follow this for 4km, mainly on the east bank, below the steep, craggy west face of Aonach Mor. Pass a deer fence, two small dams and some deep pools en route.

Head up the broad ridge on large blocks and stable scree. Follow the ridge throughout on rough red granite. The best fun is to be had by keeping to the crest. The main pinnacle is not difficult. There are big drops on the right but easy ground on the left. The rock is more shattered near the top. Reach the summit in less than an hour from the floor of the glen.

41

The East Ridge of Carn Dearg Meadhonach (Route 12)

Either descend down the north-west shoulder of the mountain or make a day of it by traversing the main summit and continuing round the arête to Ben Nevis.

*   *   *

THE AONACHS

The two mighty mountains east of Carn Mor Dearg are called Aonach Mor and Aonach Beag. The latter despite its name *(small height)* is the higher of the two and the highest schistose mountain in the land. Its famous north-east ridge gives a rock climb just outside the scope of this book, but its complex north-east face is generally disappointing from a scrambling point of view. It is probably of more interest to botanists on account of its large band of limestone.

Aonach Mor has some good walking on its east ridge, but its main attraction for scramblers lies in An Cul Choire *(the rear corrie)* on its south-east flank, where schist is in contact with granite. Both rocks are very sound at this junction and some good scrambling can be had on an apron of baked schist below a narrow granite ridge -

the Aonach Seang *(slender ridge)*. The ridge itself is a rock climb (Severe for a short section), but this can easily be avoided by going up the hillside on the right.

The long and devious approaches to An Cul Choire will deter many. The shortest route is from the Glen Nevis car park over the Bealach Cumhann, up Coire Giubhsachan and over the bealach between Aonach Beag and Aonach Mor - the last stage involving a descent of more than 350m. Another approach is through the Nevis gorge and over the bealach between Aonach Beag and Sgurr Choinnich Beag, then across An Coire Calma. The scrambling alone does not justify such effort, but those visiting this remote part of the range for the first time will have reward enough in the wild surroundings.

13. HEADWALL OF AN CUL CHOIRE   Grade 3   *

The route tries to follow as closely as possible a straight, narrow cleft containing a very small stream, which is in direct line with the prominent ridge higher up. Start at the first mass of rock left of a deep gully cut into earth and boulders (G.R. 198 724). Weave a way to and fro up this, move right across the stream and head up a grassy runnel past a large slab. Then move back left up large steps to the top of the slab.

Continue upwards and break out onto much easier-angled rock slabs. Go up these pleasantly to the first big groove which trends up left slightly. Ascend this past a long large block and then clamber over a smaller wedged flake above. Stride left across the wall at the obvious break and move some distance left to the front of the buttress.

Pass two grooves and trend up left to reach the slot with the small stream which points the way. Stay on the right side of this. There is one awkward move at the first rock step. Then follow delightful rock with large holds until the angle eventually eases at a large grassy terrace.

When the rocks steepen on this side of the stream, cross over and ascend the easier left bounding rib. Make a short detour left to avoid a steeper section. (It is easy to walk off left here.) Regain the rib and continue to a short grassy section. Move 3m left to break through the next rock section and reach a small triangular-shaped grass patch topped by a short chimney/groove. Ascend the rocks immediately right of this on good holds.

Continue more easily up to the next mass of rock and then move right into the bed of the stream where it contains a large boulder. Scramble up the steep ground on the right-hand side of the stream and emerge on a grassy hillside. The climbers' ridge (Aonach Seang) dominates the slope on the left.

Some minor outcrops can be sought out by moving further right. Finally gain the broad south ridge of Aonach Mor at a height of 1180m. It is only a few hundred metres from here to the summit. If transport has been arranged in Leanachan Forest or at Corriechoille, a magnificent walk can be had down the east ridge from the summit which starts to swing north after a kilometre. A track can be joined just north of a waterfall and dam on the Allt Coire an Eoin.

* * *

THE GREY CORRIES

The remaining eastern half of the Ben Nevis Range is known as the Grey Corries. They consist of shattered quartzite, but make a splendid ridge walk. The only scramble of note in these hills occurs at their eastern end near an outlier called Stob Ban *(white peak)*. It is on huge slabs of compact quartzite - quite the best scramble on such rock in Lochaber, though it does become rather treacherous in the wet.

14. THE GIANT'S STAIRCASE OF COIRE CLAURIGH
Grade 2 **

A long but easy approach can be made from Coirechoille or Corrour to the bothy in the Lairig Leacah *(slabby pass)* at G.R. 282 736. The Giant's Staircase is west-south-west from here at the back of Coire Claurigh, just north of Stob Ban. There is a good view of it from Sgurr Innse, a fine hill on the east side of the Lairig Leacach.

From the bothy go up by the Allt a'Chuil Choirean and cross peat-bog to the base of the lowest slab. Climb faint cracks on the right-hand side of this, then cross a sloping grass terrace and follow another crack on the second slab. Continue easily, stringing together shorter sections of slab and trending slightly left. Reach a dip of boggy ground, marking the end of the first 'step'.

Right of centre at the start of the next step is a nose of steeper rock with a corner and weeping slab to its right. Go to the right side of the slab and follow holds up it. Move left at the top and continue up a long section of delightful rock to a huge rock terrace with a small lochan.

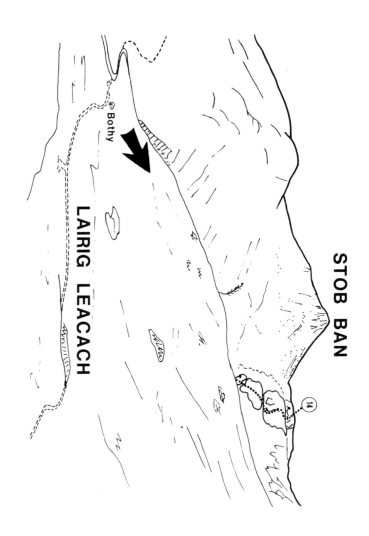

Bothy

LAIRIG LEACACH

STOB BAN

14

The strata of the third rock step are notably contorted. On the right there is a left-trending grassy gully with an easier angled slab to its right. Climb the left bounding rib of the gully and follow big steps easily up left. This last section makes a delightful contrast with the more delicate slabs below. Finish at the bealach between Stob Ban and the main ridge. There is an excellent panorama from the top of Stob Ban, worth toiling up the scree for.

*   *   *

The Loch Laggan Hills

The hills on the north side of Loch Laggan are dominated by the mighty Creag Meagaidh, a mountain well-famed for its winter climbing. However, the vegetatious cliffs of mica schist in Coire Ardair are nightmarish to climb on in the summer. The two scrambles now described are more appealing because they are on ridges which have inward dipping rock strata. Whymper took advantage of this same condition when he made the first ascent of the Matterhorn in 1865! (See his 'Scrambles Amongst the Alps').

*　　*　　*

BEINN A'CHAORAINN *(mountain of the rowan tree)*
The three tops of Beinn a' Chaorainn have vied with each other over the years for the status of highest top. On the current O.S. 1:25,000 map their heights from north to south are 1044, 1049, and 1049m respectively. The scramble is on the east ridge of the central top.

15. EAST RIDGE OF BEINN A' CHAORAINN

Grade 1　　**

The shortest approach to this ridge sits on the join of several maps. It starts where the Allt na h-Uamha meets the A86, 3km east of Laggan Dam.

Head north along the west bank of the river at G.R. 399 819. After almost 1km turn left along a fence and head up to a track. Turn right and continue up the glen through a large plantation. After the last gate go west to the foot of the ridge.

Ascend a toe protruding from the base, then walk along a leveller section to reach the main rocky part of the ridge at a height of about 800m. Move right, over some blocky scree, to gain the start of a long rock rib. Go up this and continue hunting out rock buttresses and short rock walls. The rock is flaggy granulite/schist. Narrow arête-like sections can be found in places. The best line twists to and fro and can be varied at will. Arrive on the central summit only too quickly.

A pleasant circuit can be made by going round to the Bealach a' Bharnish, up onto Creag Meagaidh, and then back down its south-west/south ridge to the starting place.

*　　*　　*

MEALL COIRE CHOILLE-RAIS

South-east of the main summit of Creag Meagaidh is a spur and small top called Meall Coire Choille-rais *(the top of the corrie of the shrub wood)*. Nestling beneath it to the north is a beautiful corrie with a large, almost circular lochan. A scramble can be made up the east ridge of the top and although not as satisfying as the previous route, it is a quick way to the plateau.

16. EAST RIDGE OF MEALL COIRE CHOILLE-RAIS
Grade 2

Start at a loop of the old road where the Allt Coire Choille-rais emerges from Moy Woods (G.R. 445 841). In moderate water conditions go up the bed of the stream on delightful slabs veined with pink and white pegmatite.

Leave the woods at a deer fence and walk up the glen passing a waterfall on the right bank. Continue up the stream, then move onto the gently sloping open hillside. Go past the ridge slightly then swing left and up to it.

Ascend steep grass and scree to the lowest rock section. There is a large grassy gully on the right. Scramble up a stepped rock rib. Before reaching a short jutting nose, traverse left along grass and go up and back right to regain rock. Continue up more broken ground. Move slightly right, then keep weaving to and fro to find the easiest line. Short rocky steps alternate with vegetated ground.

Route finding becomes a little bit more awkward towards the top, where jutting noses of rock have to be negotiated. End easily a short distance away from the top. A circuit of the corrie over Puist Coire Ardair *(the post of the high corrie)* leads back to the start.

* * *

The Ardverikie Hills

On the south side of Loch Laggan there are some lovely hills which receive attention from two different groups of hillgoers. Rock climbers flock to the cliffs of Binnein Shuas to tick off a classic Severe called Ardverikie Wall, and Munro-baggers make for Creag Pitridh and Geal Charn (Mullach Coire an Iubhair). Further north, on the east side of Lochan na h-Earba, a more modest hill - Creag a' Chuir - will be of interest to determined scramblers. It can be seen peeping over the bealach between Binnein Shuas *(upper peak)* and Binnein Shios *(lower peak)* when travelling east along the A86 in the vicinity of Moy Lodge. It is approached by a walk of several kilometres along a good estate road.

17. WEST BUTTRESS OF CREAG A' CHUIR

Grade 3 **

The shortest approach is from Kinloch Laggan, but the scramble can be combined best with a good hillwalk by starting from Moy Bridge at G.R. 432 830. Clamber over a deer fence at G.R. 434 828 and follow a track to a junction. Turn right at this and continue round to Lochan na h-Earba. Follow the track on the east side of this to another lochan of the same name. Go half way along the second lochan, then head east up the hillside to the middle of three buttresses on the west face of Creag a' Chuir. Weave between boulders and fallen trees to reach the bottom of the largest area of slabby rocks on the face.

Start near the right-bounding gully and move left up rock steps covered in pine needles. Go up to a broken rock step and ascend this to gain a leftward slanting slab. The rock is coarse crystalline pegmatite - the same as that on Binnein Shuas - and a pleasure to climb on.

When the slab steepens, move right a few metres on a grassy ledge until it is possible to gain a line slanting up left. Follow this, weaving slightly, then make a long step left (crux) and move up to a heathery niche. Exit onto easier ground with large boulders.

Slant up right and follow a broad rib of fluted rock to more boulders. Ascend a bilberry slope to a short rock buttress with an undercut roof. Scramble up the prominent groove immediately right of the steepest rock, until forced to traverse right below a slanting roof. Break back left and follow the delightful slabby rock to easier ground.

Walk towards the summit incorporating a rock wall on the way. Romp along a rib to the top – a fine viewpoint.

The south-west side can be descended easily, but enthusiasts will loop round to Sron nan Tarmachan and over Meall Buidhe to bag Geal Carn and Creag Pitridh as well.

*　　*　　*

West Buttress of Creag A'Chuir (Route 17)

Ben Alder and Geal-Chàrn

The hills to the west of Loch Ericht are among the remotest in this guide. There are no great scrambles here in summer, but any visit to the area is an experience in itself. Ben Alder is the major mountain, both in terms of bulk and height. It is reminiscent of Ben Nevis, having an extensive summit plateau (nearly 4km² over 1000m), steep north and east faces and some long narrow ridges.

All approaches are long and unless permission is obtained to drive part way along Loch Ericht from Dalwhinnie, an overnight stop in the area would be usual. Fortunately there are two bothies on opposite sides of the mountain which make convenient bases. These are Culra Bothy on the Caol Reidh *(narrow flood-plain)* below Carn Dearg at G.R. 522 761, and the supposedly haunted Ben Alder Cottage near the shore of Loch Ericht at G.R. 498 679. Approaches start from Dalwhinnie, Kinloch Laggan (via Blackburn of Pattack Bothy at G.R. 544 817), Moy Bridge on the A86, and Corrour Station (via Loch Ossian Youth Hostel). There are three bealachs on different sides of Ben Alder which allow the mountain to be circuited.

* * *

BEN ALDER

The three scrambles now described are at the northern end of Ben Alder. The first two are known as the Short Leachas and Long Leachas and although little more than walks, they do give very pleasant ways to the summit. The most convenient approach is from Culra Bothy.

18. SHORT LEACHAS   Grade 1

The eastern spur on the north ridge of Ben Alder is called the Short Leachas. *(The word leachas is derived from leth-chas meaning one leg).* It is low in its grade and gives a quick route to the plateau.

Start at the lowest mass of rock up and left from a tiny lochan. Move to the left side and scramble up to the right at first, then zig-zag to a ledge with large boulders and backed by a slabby wall. Now follow a narrow vegetated ledge slanting up left to easy ground. All this section can be avoided on the left.

A bouldery slope leads to the next rock band which is deceptively

52

Ben Alder and Sgor Iutharn from Caol Reidh (Routes 18, 19, 20, 21)

steep in the centre. There are some loose blocks in places and a variety of lines are possible. An easy way starts on the left side and ascends a grassy groove back to the crest of the buttress. There are no difficulties from here to the top. The upper section is over slivers of schistose flag, rather shattered in places. Emerge on the plateau at a height of 1060m. It is easy from here to the summit. The broad western shoulder gives an easy descent - a great place for skiing, especially in early spring.

19. LONG LEACHAS   Grade 1   *

The Long Leachas is the north-eastern spur at the end of the north ridge of Ben Alder. It is the nearest part of the mountain to Culra Bothy. Of similar grade to its partner, but slightly more interesting. It is probably best approached along the north bank of Allt a' Bhealaich Dduibh, which is then crossed in the vicinity of G.R. 507 746.

Ascend easily over several minor tops to where the ridge steepens at about 760m. Go up to a broken rock band, with a prominent groove/crack left of centre. This can be avoided by grassy steps to left or right. Taken direct it gives a steep pitch of Grade 3.

Continue easily over a col and along an easy grass ridge to the next steepening. Weave to and fro up grassy steps hunting out small rock outcrops as required. Go along a bouldery section of ridge to a narrowing at a col.

Go up the jumbled mass of blocks on the other side to a short section of shattered rock pinnacles. Further boulders and shattered rock cover the undulating top part of the ridge as it merges with the summit plateau.

After visiting the summit, a quick route back to Culra Bothy is to descend the Short Leachas and join a path on the east bank of the Allt 'a Bhealaich Bheithe. The south-east ridge can be descended by those making for Ben Alder Cottage.

There is a hanging corrie to the north of Ben Alder's Summit which holds snow until late in the year. On the west side of the stream that drains this corrie there is a prominent rock buttress which gives some interesting scrambling. The rock is better than on the first two routes, because the buttress is at right angles to them and has inward-dipping strata. Approach from the path along the Allt a' Bhealaich Dhuibh.

20. NORTH BUTTRESS Grade 2/3 *

Where the stream tumbles down the north face there are some picturesque little waterfalls. To the right of these are some large slabs, and right again and slightly higher is a rock nose at the start of the buttress proper. Move around to the right of the rock nose and head up beside an orange/red-stained rock wall. Reach a grassy terrace which leads left to the centre of the buttress. An ascent of this part of the buttress is problematical and is only for climbers. So head up by a second section of wall until just below a third wall which lies back slightly.

A short rock ramp and crack lead left from here to the centre of the buttress. Find a hold for the right foot and using a good jug on the ramp, jam the left foot in the crack and so gain a grassy continuation of the ramp. Head up this until it levels. Once on the crest of the buttress, turn right and climb sound slabby rock to a flatter grassy section.

The buttress now steepens, but the scrambling is very good and can be varied at will. The best line is on the crest or just right of it.

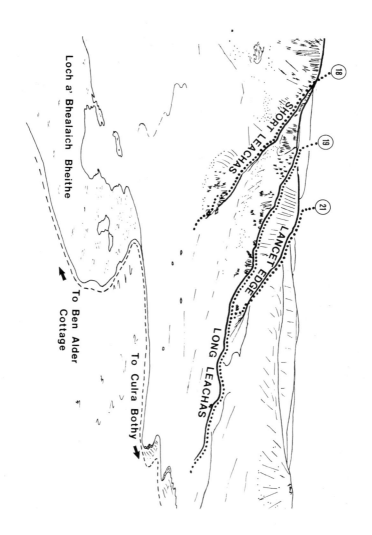

Loch a' Bhealaich Bheithe

To Ben Alder
Cottage

To Culra Bothy

LONG LEACHAS

LANCET EDGE

SHORT LEACHAS

18

19

21

The rough rock is delightful. A corrugated slabby wall with a small corner in the middle gives a pleasant finale, before the buttress levels out and merges with the plateau. Head up the corrie to the summit, or move slightly right and follow the right-bounding shoulder instead.

*   *   *

GEAL-CHÀRN

There is a chain of varied hills across the Bealach Dubh from Ben Alder. The central mountain, Geal-Chàrn is almost as large as Ben Alder. Its summit is an extensive plateau, and its north-east face is divided by a narrow ridge on either side of which are large lochs nestling in deep corries. At the eastern end of the mountain, directly across from the Long Leachas, is a soaring narrow ridge called the Lancet Edge. It rises to a top on the eastern shoulder which is un-named on the O.S. 1:50,000 map, but known as Sgor Iutharn *(peak of hell)*. It is an obvious feature from Culra Bothy.

21. THE LANCET EDGE OF SGOR IUTHARN Grade 1 *

This is a surprisingly easy route in summer and hardly merits it grade unless the bottom section is included as described.

If approaching from Culra Bothy, leave the Bealach Dubh path where it turns away from the Allt Loch an Sgoir at G.R. 501 745. Head up to steep rock at the base of the ridge. Find a tongue of slabs on the left-hand side, with an overhanging wall above and left. Ascend the slabs to a grass terrace. Avoid a steeper section above by heading diagonally right. Then traverse a heathery ledge rightwards. Move up on heather and reach a slabby rock rib further right. Ascend the corrugated rock and continue easily up heather and some boulders to the broad crest of the ridge.

Some distance higher, further rock outcrops occur. Move across right to the most continuous of these. Start up easy steps, then go slightly left and follow a rocky rib which eventually degenerates into boulders. This is rather artificial, but better than going up steep grass.

After a flatter section head up left to another rock rib. Gain this from the left and wander up the steep broken arête. Continue easily up grass and boulders to a slightly narrower part of the ridge. Ascend a broken rock band on the crest. More grassy slope leads to a tiny col where the ridge narrows considerably and becomes more rocky. From here to the summit is very pleasant but easy. The ridge consists of frost-shattered flaggy schist and the best fun is to be had by hopping along the rocks exactly on the crest. There are superb views. The ridge flattens out suddenly at the summit of Sgor Iutharn.

To complete a fine circuit, pick off the summit of Geal-Chàrn which is two kilometres away, and then descend the Aisre Ghobhain. Care is needed to locate the latter in bad visibility. Then head over Diollaid a' Chairn to Carn Dearg and descend its steep eastern side back to Culra Bothy.

* * *

*'The Ring of Steall' - Coire A'Mhail viewed from Aonach Beag
(Route 24)*

THE SOUTHERN
GROUP

This group, which includes the Glencoe hills, has as much scrambling
as all the other groups put together. Since the approaches to the
scrambles here are also relatively short, it is no wonder that the area
is so popular.

The Mamores

On the south side of Glen Nevis is a superb range of hills, which but for their proximity to Ben Nevis would attract much more attention. A walk along the main ridge gives as fine an outing as any in the area and includes a satisfying tally of Munros.

Mullach nan Coirean *(the summit of the little corrie)* is a broad granite peak at the western end of the range. Below its east face is the little frequented Coire Dearg *(red corrie)*. There is a minor scramble in the southern lobe of the corrie which might be of interest to those making a circuit if the corrie.

It is possible to approach it by the Allt a' Choire Dheirg from Achriabhach, but there is no path to speak of and the ground is rather wet. A pleasant outing is to be had by starting up the north-east ridge of Mullach nan Coirean, going round Coire Dearg and descending the north ridge of Stob Ban. The scramble can be included by making a small diversion halfway round. Three contrasting rocks are encountered during the circuit - red granite on Mullach nan Coirean, white quartzite on the top few metres of ridge near G.R. 138 657, and greenish grey mica schist on the north ridge of Stob Ban.

22. THE GENDARME RIDGE OF COIRE DEARG
Grade 3   *

Start from Achriabhach and follow a forestry track to a junction. Turn sharp left and then go up a fire break (G.R. 137 684), heading steeply south-westwards up the hillside. Emerge from the forest and eventually join a wire fence on the north-east ridge of Mullach nan Coirean. Go over the rocky summit and continue round to the next top which is almost flat enough and grassy enough to be a football pitch. Shortly after this the ridge narrows and drops to a low point of 880m. About 200m further on (G.R. 136 655) a shattered granite ridge comes up from the corrie on the left. There are scree-filled gullies on either side of it. Either descend the western gully or slant down from near the 880m col, to the foot of the ridge.

Omit the broken rocks at the bottom. Gain the first section of more continuous rock, by moving along a grassy ledge from the scree on the right. Weave a way up on rough red granite until a steeper section is reached. Avoid this by traversing round to the left near a protruding finger of rock. Regain the crest by climbing the obvious steep break and moving right at the top.

Continue up the crest to another steepening and turn this on the left. Follow the broken rocks more easily to the top. Rejoin the main ridge and walk along to the north top of Stob Ban. Descend the north ridge and move left near the end to avoid the steep nose. Arrive back at the starting point.

* * *

STOB BAN

Stob Ban is a shapely peak - one of the the most prominent in Glen Nevis. However it is a more complex mountain than it appears from afar. The north-east face is made up of several buttresses and gullies, and there are two small northern tops. The main peak consists of shattered quartzite, hence its name *(white peak)*, but the northern tops are of mica schist. There has been some confusion over the years about the names of the main buttresses.

The mass of rock directly below the summit, and split by two large gullies, is known as South Buttress. The huge triangular face, north-north-east of the summit at G.R. 149 657, is the lower part of Central Buttress. The more southerly of the two northern tops is on the main Mamore ridge and has a height of 912m. The other north top is slightly lower and is 150m along the north spur of the mountain. The broken ridge which runs north-east from this last top is known as North Buttress, and it gives a good scramble with some interesting route finding. It was first ascended in 1895, but has been surprisingly neglected since.

23. NORTH BUTTRESS   Grade 3   **

Start from the Lower Falls in Glen Nevis and follow a path up the east bank of the Allt Coire a' Mhusgain. Pass through some rather open woodland and then ascend a series of steep zig-zags on the flank of Sgurr a' Mhaim. Continue along the path for 300m or so, crossing several minor streams. Then drop down to the floor of Coire Mhusgain *(rotting corrie),* and ascend a grassy arête between two streams on the other side. Cross a small gap and staying right of the stream go past a small waterfall.

When the angle eases slightly, head hard right (north-west) over undulating grassy ground, rather boggy in places. Cross a boulder slope to reach a grassy terrace jutting from the base of the North Buttress. There are fine views down Glen Nevis from here.

The first part of the route is not well defined. The most prominent feature is a leftward slanting scree gully. Right of this is a small

60

The East Ridge of the North Top of Stob Ban (Route 23)

vegetated buttress, and right again is a much smaller more vegetated gully. Go up to a tiny slabby buttress immediately right of the latter. Ascend a slabby tongue of rock at first and then move to the left side of steeper rock above. Continue up a rocky rib until this peters out. Go up a short stretch of scree and then move left up a bilberry covered slope to the first buttress proper.

The buttress is climbed by a diagonal line, starting at the lowest rocks in the centre and finishing at the top left-hand corner. The last part involves a short step down, before easier ground is reached.

Go straight up to a rock tower formed from two huge perched blocks. Move up between two small trees on the right-hand side of the tower. Ignore the obvious gully formed by erosion of an orange dyke. Instead move left and reach the gap between the back of the tower and the neighbouring rock wall. Bridge up this with difficulty (crux). Go up to another short rock wall and climb a recess, exiting leftwards.

Move up to another section of steep rock. Go round to the left of a jutting corner, and eventually regain the crest at a small recess just

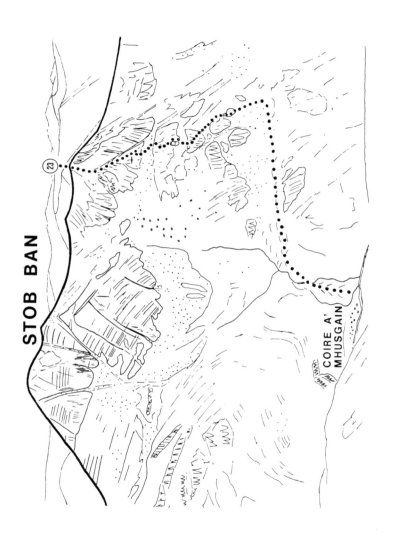

STOB BAN

COIRE A' MHUSGAIN

right of a small rowan tree. Head across slightly right and ascend a broken recess of orange dyke rock. Move right near the top and gain a bilberry covered ledge. Follow the continuation of the dyke to a large grassy terrace.

Descend very slightly, cross some boulders, and go up to the centre of the next rock band. Climb a vegetated, left-trending recess and at the first opportunity move onto a ledge on the right. Wriggle up into a small chimney in the wall on the right. Continue more easily to the next mass of rock. Either ascend this left of centre with some difficulty or avoid it easily on the right.

Continue up the crest of the broken twisting arête. A large gully is now visible on the right. Move to the left side of a small nose of rock and then walk along a short level section of ridge. Reach a rock pinnacle which blocks the way. Move to the left side of this and ascend a slabby wall using large horizontal cracks. Pull up onto the ridge crest beside a large jutting flake.

Continue along the crest of the ridge, over perched boulders, to another steepening. Go up by a leftward slanting recess to a short section of spiky arête. A grassy slope leads to the summit.

Descend the north ridge of Stob Ban, keeping left at the end, back to the Lower Falls.

24. THE RING OF STEALL   Grade 1   **ʰ

The circuit of Coire a' Mhail is mainly a long, exhilarating ridge walk with only very short sections of easy scrambling. It is best done anti-clockwise to avoid problems in descent. The outing starts and finishes from Steall Cottage, on the south side of the Nevis Gorge. Approach from the top car park in Glen Nevis as for Route 5. Cross the wire bridge to Steall Cottage.

The first part of the outing is the most difficult and the least pleasant. It requires fairly determined 'Tarzan tactics'. The problem is to reach the floor of Coire nan Cnamh *(corrie of the bones),* which is hidden behind the north-east ridge of Sgurr a' Mhaim *(peak of the large round hill).* A way has to be found up the steep wooded hillside due south of Steall Cottage, midway between An Steall on the left and a prominent crag in the trees on the right.

The best line stays near to the right (west) bank of a small stream. At times it is necessary to traverse to and fro some distance to circumvent awkward rock steps. Most of the terrain is steep heather

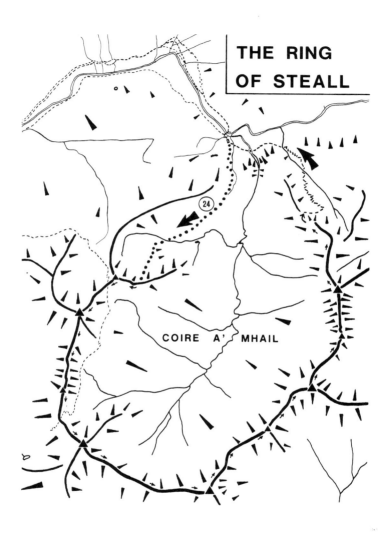

THE RING
OF STEALL

COIRE A' MHAIL

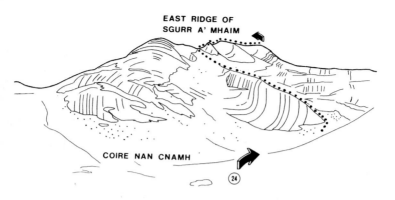

EAST RIDGE OF SGURR A' MHAIM

COIRE NAN CNAMH

(24)

and grass. Eventually the angle eases and the source of the small stream is reached above the trees. The Allt Coire a' Mhail can be seen down on the left.

Head south-south-west over undulating ground to the floor of Coire nan Cnamh. Spectacular folding can be seen in the quartzite strata at the back of the corrie. The left bounding ridge of the corrie is the east ridge of Sgurr a' Mhaim. The first part of the ridge above Sron Coire nan Cnamh is not very interesting, but the route joins this ridge further up.

Walk across the floor of the corrie to the right-hand end of the wall of contorted quartzite. Go round the back of this and so gain the crest of the rock band. Scramble up this on good rock and continue up steep grass to reach the east ridge of Sgurr a' Mhaim at G.R. 170 670. See diagram on P.63.

Go up the ridge to the 'bad step'. This involves just one slightly exposed stride. It is trivial in good conditions, but can be unnerving on a windy day. Then head up left to regain the crest of the ridge. Swing round to the right and continue to a small top at a height of about 965m.

The ridge now turns to the left and after 100m an amazing stalker's path crosses the ridge at a slight col (956m). Those wishing to miss out the summit of Sgurr a' Mhaim can follow this path southwards and then cut across right to gain the south ridge of the mountain. The path virtually encircles Sgurr a' Mhaim and makes an interesting outing in its own right.

The south ridge of Sgurr a' Mhaim, leading to Sgor an Iubhair

(1001m), is known as *'The Devil's Ridge'*. It is exciting in winter, but much tamer in summer. The first gap is the deepest, but is easy to descend. A short slab on the other side gives some slight interest. Further on, another dip in the ridge gives more fun. Stay on the crest and make two strides (or one jump and then a stride!) onto large orange blocks where a dyke cuts across the ridge. If the day or the party is too windy an easy way can be found below on the right side of the ridge.

Go along the pleasant narrow ridge to a small top called Stob a' Choire Mhail. Continue to the summit of Sgor an Iubhair *(peak of the yew tree)*. This Munro is unnamed on all O.S. maps, but has a spot height of 1001m. Follow the ridge round to Am Bodach. Descend carefully on steep muddy scree to a bealach. Go over a small top on the ridge and reach Stob Coire a' Chairn. Do not continue east from here, but return from the summit cairn a short distance and descend the north ridge to Bealach a' Chadha Riabhaich *(col of the grey pass)*.

The summits of An Garbhanach and An Gearanach are incorrectly marked on all O.S. maps. An Garbhanach is the southern top of a north-south section of ridge. It is marked by a height of 975m at G.R. 188 665. An Gearanach is the northern top of the same section of ridge, and is marked by a height of 982m at G.R. 187 669.

The traverse of An Garbhanach provides some of the best scrambling of the day. Keep to the crest of a shattered arête with a path on the left. Stay on the crest when the path moves over to the right. The rock now improves slightly. The ridge levels out and one large block has conspicuous crampon scratches on it. The going becomes easy again by the time the col is reached between An Garbhanach and An Gearanach.

The descent from An Gearanach requires care if visibility is bad. Go north to start with and then descend a shoulder north-westwards to a slight flattening at G.R. 184 677. Now traverse east into the top of Coire Chadha Chaoruinn and pick up a path which zig-zags down to the floor of Glen Nevis. Continue round below An Steall back to Steall Cottage.

*   *   *

SAMUEL'S CAVE

On the opposite side of the glen from the top car park in Glen Nevis, there is a rock outcrop which has split in two to form a deep cleft. The outcrop is at exactly the same height as the car park and due south of it. The cleft is known as Uamh Shomhairle *(Samuel's Cave)*, and it provides an entertaining diversion on an indifferent day. The entrance can be hard to locate on a first visit. It is normally approached from the footbridge at G.R. 158 684.

*   *   *

COIRE A' MHAIL

The 'Lost Valley' in Glen Coe is a very famous glen, and a popular walk. There is a glen in the Mamores which is bigger than the Lost Valley and yet more difficult to enter. Many people marvel at the spectacular waterfall called An Steall which issues from the mouth of the glen, many walkers scamper along the surrounding ridges, but relatively few visit the floor of the glen itself. The head of the glen is called Coire a' Mhail *(corrie of rent)*. It is a classic example of a hanging valley.

*   *   *

Glencoe

For those driving north on the A82, the bleakness of Rannoch Moor serves only to emphasise the dramatic scenery of Glencoe. As the road drops down through the glen itself, the mountains seem to soar higher on each side. With so many buttresses, ridges, faces and corries in proximity, it is a unique area for hillgoers. There is something here for everyone - walkers, scramblers and climbers - and all reasonably close to the road. The rock is nearly all of volcanic origin, and the best of it is superb for scrambling.

The Glencoe area is usually regarded as extending to the turn off for Glen Etive, even though Buachaille Etive Mor is the wrong side of the watershed. The scrambles on the north side of the A82 are described first.

North Glencoe

The north side of Glencoe is dominated by one long, switch-back ridge - the famous Aonach Eagach. There are several ridges in the area which are higher and longer, but none which are so narrow and so difficult to escape from once committed. It is a very popular excursion, and can be thoroughly recommended to those with a head for heights. Some sections are extremely exposed. This makes it a difficult outing to grade, because the technical difficulties are not great.

*   *   *

25. THE AONACH EAGACH   Grade 2   ***

The ridge is normally traversed from east to west, and transport at both ends saves a long walk up the glen. Purists start from Altnafeadh and ascend the Devil's Staircase. Scramblers start from 'The Study' and include a route on A' Chailleach (the next one described in this guide). The masses start from Allt-na-ruigh and follow the south-east shoulder of Am Bodach. The latter start is now described.

From a parking bay some 300m west of Allt-na-ruigh (G.R. 173 567) follow an obvious path up the hillside. Leave the path where it starts to traverse round beside the Allt Ruigh at a height of 450m. Instead, head north-west and find some enjoyable scrambling on the shoulder of Am Bodach. Continue up the broader ridge above and reach the dog-legged summit. The other starts reach this point from the other side.

The descent from Am Bodach is an early test of nerve. It can be the most difficult part of the traverse in winter, and parties often retreat from this point. Soon after the summit, the ridge starts to narrow. Descend exposed ledges on the right side of the crest. Then drop down left by a large boulder just before a small rock tower. Large, well worn steps lead to a fence post and easier going. Trend left and descend some steeper, more shattered rock with care. Move back right and go down a short section of slab to another iron fence post and much easier ground.

Follow the path along the undulating ridge dotted with fence posts. Reach a small top (924m), then turn right and descend loose rock to a col with a big scree gully on the left. Continue easily to the broad summit of Meall Dearg. The rock here is rather different from the volcanic lavas which make up much of the ridge. It consists of pink porphyrite which was intruded along the boundary-fault of the Glencoe cauldron.

Leave the summit and cross back into the 'cauldron'. The next section of ridge is again made of rhyolite and andesite lavas. It is very narrow and exposed in places, and from here to the col before Stob Coire Leith is the best part of the traverse. This is the genuine Aonach Eagach *(notched ridge)* as marked on O.S. maps.

Follow the ridge easily at first, then descend leftwards by some stunted pinnacles and bridge pleasantly up a gully the other side of the dip. Continue along the easy ridge with some short rock steps. Eventually make a rightwards descent on rocks immediately left of a short gully (or descend the gully itself). Go past a broken pinnacle to a col and then scramble up a clean, slabby rock step on the left side of a square tower.

Continue over a short section of red-stained rock (sub-aerially weathered lava) to some small pinnacles. Either go over these and make an awkward descent from the last one, or avoid them on the left. Continue more easily along a stony path. Move right to some large flakes and descend long rock steps. Balance along a short rocky arête (or avoid it on the left), and then ascend slightly.

The next section consists of a series of rock pinnacles, separated by small gaps. There are big drops on both sides. This is the most exposed part of the ridge. The rock is good and the holds are well worn. Ascent directly from the last gap is difficult, and a slightly easier option on the right is usually taken.

The ridge is now level for a short section. Then make a long twisting descent, interspersed with minor rises, to a narrow col. Awkward sloping steps lead up from here out of the 'cauldron'. After one more narrow section, follow a twisting path on quartzite rock to the summit of Stob Coire Leith *(peak of the grey corrie)*.

The ridge presents no difficulties from here to the summit of Sgorr nam Fiannaidh. The rock is nearly all quartzite with occasional dykes and small outcrops of porphyrite, which are obvious because of their pink/orange colour.

By far the safest descent from the western end of the ridge is to head north-west to the col below the Pap of Glencoe. Then turn left and meet the road to Glencoe village near the Youth Hostel. It is also possible to descend the west bank of Clachaig Gully, but this requires careful mapwork or prior knowledge if it is to be identified from above. In any case the path is very loose and steep, and there is a danger of dislodged stones falling onto climbers in the gully. Some parties prefer to reverse the whole ridge!

There are no safe descent routes on the south side of the ridge between Am Bodach and Stob Coire Leith.

*   *   *

A'CHAILLEACH

At the eastern end of the Aonach Eagach, on the opposite side of Coire an Ruigh from Am Bodach *(the old man),* is a jutting shoulder of rock called A' Chailleach *(the old woman).* A very enjoyable scramble can be had on the hillside leading up to this point by stringing together a host of slabs and small outcrops. The band of orange rhyolite near the top is a prominent feature from many parts of the glen, and it makes a superb and spectacular finish to the route.

26. THE SOUTH FACE OF A' CHAILLEACH

Grade 2/3   **

Park in a small bay in the rock cutting below 'The Study' at G.R. 182 563, or on the other side of the road at a waterfall a little further up the glen. Head up slightly left to the old road, and cross it near a large cairn with good views of the glen. 'The Study' is a corruption of the Scots word 'stiddie' meaning anvil. The original Gaelic name An t-Innean *(the anvil)* refers to a large flat-topped rock near here, but exactly which one is not clear.

Go up a faint path to a prominent dark rock face and scramble easily up the short right-hand end. A small climbing hut is immediately on the right. Walk across slightly left over a shallow col to the first of a series of pink rhyolite slabs. Follow these, and some short walls, up the hillside until they fade out. Move left across a tiny stream and head up to an outcrop of steeper, darker andesite. There is a small tree to the left of a long, narrow overhang. Left again there is a wide recess of red dyke rock. Climb this by some large slabby steps and move right at the top to a ledge. Continue straight up more easily.

When the rocks steepen again, trend right and make an awkward move to gain a niche with two jammed boulders. Exit by a difficult step up to a ledge at the top.

Reach easier purple-stained rock, and slant leftwards up a rocky rib. Move across right to the next section and scramble up right of a shallow gully. Cross a small dip and head up grass and scree to the next rock band.

The right-hand section is too steep, so move up to the centre of the left-hand half. Follow a staircase rightwards past a small jutting block to a large boulder on a ledge. Ascend the wall behind this, then slant up leftwards.

Cross easy ground to a rather mossy buttress. Scramble up the right bounding edge on purple rock. Continue on grassy ledges, and then ascend the easier right-hand end of a short overhanging wall. Go up more broken ground, slanting left, then cross a bouldery slope to the next rock buttress.

Start at the lowest rocks and scramble up to a small rightward sloping ramp. Move up this with difficulty, then go left 4 metres along a ledge to a mossy groove. Step out right at the top to easier ground. Continue for some distance over grass and scree to an area of broken rocks with a slabby wall above.

Move up to the shorter and easier left-hand side near a square-cut block. Ascend a short wall and zig-zag up to a leftward trending slab which leads to easier ground. Head up rightwards over grassy terrain to the middle of a large steep wall of orange rhyolite.

Now comes the exciting part. Start from a small rock platform below the right-most of three rightward slanting grooves. Ascend the groove using surprisingly good holds. Pull up onto a ledge with a large perched boulder - a superb little pitch.

Do not go straight up from here. Instead move right past the boulder, step up slightly and continue rightwards in an exposed position to a break. Ascend this and continue scrambling on magnificent rock for some distance. Reach the top of A'Chailleach all too soon.

Head up to the crest of the ridge. From here a left turn leads over Sron Gharbh to the Aonach Eagach. A right turn leads to an unnamed top of 903m. Descend from this by continuing along the ridge to a col at 788m. Then head south off the ridge and join the shoulder which runs south-westwards, on the east side of the Allt Coire Meannarclach. Cross the stream lower down. Traverse across to the old road and so return to the starting place.

*　　*　　*

STOB BEINN A' CHRULAISTE

One kilometre east of Altnafeadh, on the south face of Stob Beinn a' Chrulaiste *(the point of the rocky mountain)*, there are some slabby, vegetated buttresses, which give surprisingly good scrambles. They are handy for those staying in Lagangarbh, and give fine views of Buachaille Etive Mor.

27. SUMMIT BUTTRESS   Grade 1/2   *

The broad buttress immediately right of the most obvious gully on the face, leads directly to the summit of the Stob. Leave the main road in the vicinity of G.R. 229 559, and slant up the hillside to the large, dry gully. Go up some slabs in the gully bed and then ascend heather on the right bank. When rock steps develop follow them, until it is possible to start working out rightwards to the centre of the buttress on a series of very pleasant rock slabs. The line can be varied easily and the rock is very sound. Weave to and fro slightly all the way up the buttress. There is some loose rock on ledges towards the top. The angle eases some distance below the summit.

28. SPLIT BUTTRESS   Grade 1   *

The narrower buttress to the right of Summit Buttress, is split by a prominent groove running from bottom right to top left. This scramble goes most of the way up the left-hand half and then transfers to the right-hand half near the top.

Go steeply up the hillside to a slab some distance below the buttress proper. Scramble pleasantly straight up the slab and then continue up more vegetated ground above. Reach the next rocky section and pick out the most satisfying line. The rock is rather more jagged and shattered than on the previous route, but loose rock is easy to spot. There are plenty of holds.

Keep position on the left-hand half of the buttress, sometimes moving close to the gully on the left. Near the top at a short heathery slope, traverse easily right and finish up the steep final section of the right-hand half of the buttress. This is delightful and covered in large holds. Emerge on a grassy slope a short distance east of the summit.

Descend the west ridge as for the previous route.

*   *   *

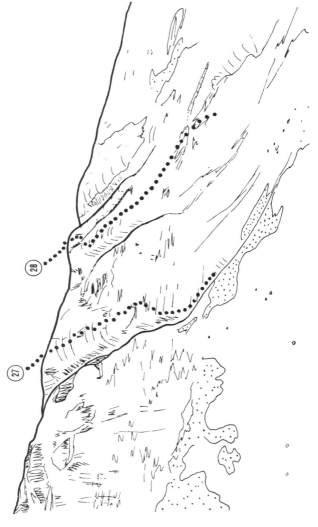

STOB BEINN A' CHRULAISTE

South Glencoe

There is a remarkable contrast between the opposite sides of Glencoe. The north side comprises one long ridge parallel to the road, whereas the south side is dissected into several major ridges, corries and glens running at right angles to the road. The ends of three ridges which project dramatically into the glen are known as 'The Three Sisters'.

The scrambles on the south side of Glencoe are now described from west to east. There are some magnificent routes here, most of them on superb rhyolite.

STOB COIRE NAM BEITH

The conical mass of Stob Coire nam Beith *(point above the corrie of the birch trees)* can be seen from the road by looking south from the western end of Loch Achtriochtan. It is tucked away in the back of Coire nam Beith, (marked as Coire nam Beitheach on O.S. maps). Not far behind it on the left is the summit of Bidean nam Bian *(the jagged summit of the hides or skins),* at 1150m the highest mountain in Argyll.

There is a small car park at the turn-off for the Clachaig Inn. Go across to the south-western end of the road bridge over the River Coe, and follow a path on the west bank of the Allt Coire nam Beith, (marked as Allt Coire nam Beitheach on O.S. maps). High up in the glen, take a left fork to reach the boulder-strewn floor of the main corrie below the rocks of Stob Coire nam Beith.

The two routes now described are both fairly difficult. They converge at a terrace 100m below the actual summit.

29. NUMBER 1 BUTTRESS   Grade 3(S)   *

Slant up some distance to the most obvious gully splitting the left-hand half of the face. This is Arch Gully. On its left is a buttress which is recessed slightly from the main face, and split from top to bottom by a narrow chimney. It is known as Number 1 Buttress. (The buttress further left is called Zero Buttress.) The chimney is an eroded dyke. There is a large terrace at one third height.

Start 5m left of Arch Gully and ascend an orange rock step on very good holds. The angle soon eases and grass leads to the beginning of the buttress proper.

Either climb the wall mid-way between Arch Gully and the dyke chimney, or slant up left from a large block further right. Continue up an easy slab, trending left, to the right-hand side of the chimney. Scramble easily up beside this on superb rock, interspersed with small mossy ledges. Reach a large sloping scree terrace.

The route now starts to move away from the dyke. The next section requires careful route finding. From a point about half way between Arch Gully and the dyke, pull up into a grassy recess. Move up left at first, then step right and make a long stretch to a hidden jug hold, which allows a slabby niche to be gained. Exit from this by stepping up high with the left foot, and soon reach easier ground. An easier option to all this starts much closer to Arch Gully, but it is more vegetated.

Continue up through a series of rocky steps and arrive at a sloping terrace, with easy ground on the left and steeper rock on the right. Head up slightly right towards the steeper rock, and make for a prominent jutting block. Reach a narrow ramp, which slants up leftwards immediately below the small roof formed by the block.

The next section is sustained and would be difficult to retreat from. Move up the ramp with difficulty, and reach a small recess. Step left again and move up into a tapering mossy niche. Go up this, then step right and make an exposed move around a slight bulge. Traverse right to a grassy ledge and take a breather.

Move up by a small perched flake and continue up to an obvious weakness. Follow this to the top.

There are no difficulties from here to the summit of Stob Coire nam Beith. It is easy then to continue round to the summit of Bidean nam Bian. However a quick descent can be made from the top of the scramble by slanting up left slightly at first, to a horizontal shelf. Go left along this, then descend the grassy shoulder above Zero Buttress. Move right near the bottom and drop down to the floor of the corrie. Curve round to the left, back to the foot of the route.

30. NUMBER 3 BUTTRESS   Grade 3   ***

This very enjoyable route finds a way up the centre of the face, between two gullies, (Central Gully on the left and Deep-Cut Chimney on the right). It starts at an obvious triangular mass of orange rock, above and left of a large scree slope.

Climb up from the lowest rocks on good holds, trending right. Make a steep pull up a wall to get back left. Continue more easily until a squat pedestal gives some more interest. This point overlooks

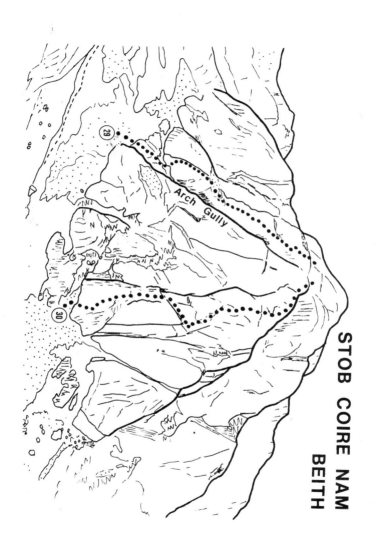

Arch Gully

STOB COIRE NAM
BEITH

Central Gully.

Reach an obvious slabby ramp slanting up right. Go along this and make some exposed moves round the corner, with good views of Deep-Cut Chimney. Keep slanting up right until it is possible to break back left slightly to reach a good ledge. The major difficulties are now over, but a lot of very good scrambling still remains.

Easier ground can be reached by walking round the left end of the ledge. Directly above the wall is too difficult, but more fun can be had by moving left, and then following a narrow ramp back right up across the wall.

Reach easier angled rock and scramble delightfully for some distance. Trend up left to the apex of the buttress. Either continue to the summit of Stob Coire nam Beith, or traverse across the depression at the top of Arch Gully to the top of Number 1 Buttress, and descend as for that route.

* * *

AONACH DUBH

The most western of the Three Sisters is called Aonach Dubh *(black height)*. The lower portion of the mountain consists of rather vegetated andesite and basalt lavas which are unattractive from a scrambling point of view. However, lying on top of these dark coloured lavas, there are flows of orange coloured rhyolite which are superb for scrambling. The junction between the two lavas is very obvious even from the road, and it can be traced easily across the western and northern sides of the mountain.

The west face of Aonach Dubh is a very spectacular side of the mountain. It can be seen when driving east from Onich, and there is a particularly fine view of it from the Clachaig Inn. It is split by six main gullies and two scoops into seven different buttresses. These are all known by letters, starting with A on the left and finishing with G on the right, although A Buttress is more commonly known as Dinner Time Buttress. (See diagram on page 80)

Only Dinner-time Buttress and B Buttress give reasonable ascents of the lower part of the face. The transition from andesite to rhyolite occurs at a natural traverse line known as Middle Ledge. One hundred metres higher, there is a broader ledge called The Rake.

All sorts of combinations of routes can be worked out on the west face. A very long traverse to and from the north face can be made to look at Ossian's Cave. It is also easy to traverse from the top of F

78

The West Face of Aonach Dubh, Glencoe (Routes 31, 32 33)

Buttress across into Coire nam Beith and then do a scramble on Stob Coire nam Beith. All the routes are approached as for Stob Coire nam Beith, along the west bank of the Allt Coire nam Beith, which is then crossed in the vicinity of G.R. 139 560. Head up the steep grassy hillside by a dilapidated wire fence.

31. DINNER-TIME BUTTRESS   Grade 1

This buttress is not as good or as hard as it looks from the road. The lower part is vegetatious, and the rock when it appears is rather loose. However it is a very direct route up the face, and the scrambling on the rhyolite at the top is short but pleasant. It also serves as a convenient approach to the next scramble in the guide.

The band of rhyolite is ascended in the centre, starting up a prominent narrow gully and then transferring to rocks on the right. The angle soon eases and a number of different lines can be followed. The summit of Aonach Dubh can be reached by heading up left slightly. The upper part of Number 2 Gully broadens into a small coire, and this can be crossed to reach The Rake which is described as part of the next scramble.

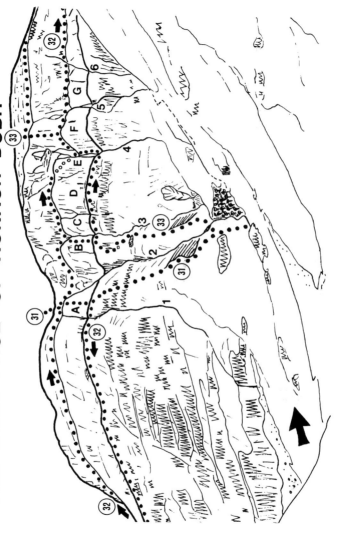

THE WEST FACE OF AONACH DUBH

32. RHYOLITE ROMP   Grade 1 **

This monster traverse line is mainly walking, but it does give superb views of the glen. Start from the base of the rhyolite band on Dinnertime Buttress and traverse left across Number 1 Gully. Keep traversing for 900m, descending slightly all the time. Eventually reach a gully which falls steeply to the floor of the glen. Go across the loose slope on the other side of this, and then look back south west. There are two parallel sloping shelves, slanting up across the north face. (This point can also be reached directly from the floor of the glen by ascending the buttress on the east bank of the gully.)

The upper shelf is not so easy to see from here, but it slants up below the dark gash of Ossian's Cave. Reaching the cave itself involves a tricky climb on vegetatious rock, (Ossian's Ladder, 60m Difficult). The climb is not recommended, and in any case the floor of the cave slopes at 45°. The cave has been formed by a huge block falling out of a dyke.

The lower shelf gives better views of the cave, and it merges with the upper shelf higher up. Go across to the trough on the left side of the lower shelf and ascend by a tiny stream on the right side of a huge boulder. Walk over boulders in the floor of the trough until it is possible to traverse out right onto the crest of the shelf. Go up this and join the upper shelf. There are fine views of the forbidding north face.

Keep traversing right below the face. Ignore the dark recess of Deep-Gash Gully, and duck down below the buttress on its right. Head across some distance to the top of Dinner-time Buttress.

Continue across Number 2 Gully and pick up a faint path which runs along a sloping terrace on the upper section of the west face. This is called The Rake. Go around the top of Number 3 gully, and continue below rock towers to a narrow horizontal ridge, with stone-covered slabs on the left. The ridge ends abruptly in a stupefying precipice.

Up on the left is a high corrie called The Amphitheatre. It is guarded by a prominent rock buttress, with steep gullies on either side. Higher up in the coire there are some large pinnacles. The one at the top right is called Winifred's Pinnacle, and the lower one on the left is called Bell's Pinnacle.

Go back along the ridge a short distance and descend the broken slabs on the right. There are a lot of loose stones here, but the descent is not unduly difficult. Traverse across Number 4 Gully and

OSSIAN'S CAVE

32

32

FROM
DINNERTIME
BUTTRESS

slant up more easily to the crest of F Buttress - a perfect vantage point for observing climbers in action on E Buttress.

Drop down over the other side of F Buttress and continue traversing across the more open face. Do not be tempted to go down any of the gullies; Eventually walk across to the floor of Coire nam Beith. Descend by the path on the west bank of the Allt Coire nam Beith.

33. B-F BUTTRESS ROUTE   Grade 2/3   *

Approach as for Dinner-time Buttress to the top of the dilapidated wire fence. Shortly after this, traverse right across Number 2 Gully and ascend steep grass for some distance. Reach a small rock band and move onto its bottom right corner from the right. Move horizontally left until able to go up easily to fine scree. Head up slightly left to a large cracked block. Ascend a slab immediately right of this, and then zig-zag up broken rock above. Reach Middle Ledge near Number 3 Gully.

It is possible to continue up the right-hand side of B Buttress by some pleasant rock ribs and so join The Rake, (see previous route). However it is more spectacular to traverse right along Middle Ledge to Number 4 Gully. This is no more than a walk, but very exposed in places.

Go over the stream in Number 4 Gully and stay below an obvious groove with a large rock flake on its right wall. Climbers go up the groove, but an easier option starts slightly further right. Go up to a small grassy ledge below a short V-groove. Instead of continuing up the groove, step right onto a large foothold, and climb up a broken rib.

Continue more easily, then ascend the left-hand of two chimneys with jammed blocks on its right wall. Follow the rib above to the headwall of the gully. The Rake can be reached by slanting up the stone-covered slabs on the left. It leads back to the top of Dinnertime Buttress, which can then be descended. A traverse up to the right leads to the crest of F Buttress. Reach this and then instead of continuing over the other side (as for the previous route), go up the grassy arête to a rock buttress. This is the South Ridge of The Amphitheatre and it constitutes the crux of the route.

Climb it either by a steep grassy groove left of centre, or by a more difficult rock rib. It gives fine views of The Amphitheatre on the left. From the top continue to the summit of Stob Coire nan Lochan, or follow a sheep track along the rim of the west face and down into Coire nam Beith.

There are several crags on the east face of Aonach Dubh, which offer climbs of all grades. The main crag is crossed by countless little ledges at its top left-hand end. This section is known as The Barn Wall, and it gives an excellent scramble.

34. BARN WALL ROUTE   Grade 2 or 3   ***

Park at a large car park (G.R.. 168 569) with a view directly up the glen between Aonach Dubh and Gearr Aonach. Follow a path to a bridge over the River Coe, then head steeply up the glen staying on the east bank of the stream. The path splits at one point, but both branches rejoin a long way up the glen near a natural rock shelter, not far above the stream. This is a good bivouac spot. It has been improved by a small stone wall.

Barn Wall is at the top left end of the crag on the opposite side of the glen at G.R. 156 558. Cross the stream and go up to the highest point on the grass slope below the face. Pull up into a small V-shaped recess (Grade 3), or follow an easy ramp which starts further right and slants back left.

Many lines are possible from here. The rock is excellent rhyolite. It is covered with large square-cut holds and the occasional jug. Zig-zag up choosing the most interesting line. Cross some intermittent heather ledges.

Eventually reach a broader heather ledge which slopes up left across the face. Go to the top left-hand end of this, passing below a steep section of rock. Find a line up less steep rocks about 9m left of an easy gully. (The Grade 2 route goes up the gully.)

Climb up on good holds, passing to the right of a large perched block. Continue up trending slightly right. Make a steep move right of a small nose, and pull up onto much easier rocks. Either carry on to the summit of Aonach Dubh, or contour round to the left and do one of the next two scrambles further up the glen.

Not far up the glen from Barn Wall is a crag known as Far Eastern Buttress. Its top left edge gives a short pleasant scramble, which is probably only of interest to those who have just completed Barn Wall Route.

35. LEFT EDGE   Grade 1/2   *

Start below the main part of the crag at some slabs which slant up to the left, (G.R. 153 555). Ascend the slabs easily and go up to the rocks at the top left side of the buttress. Follow these to the top.

The impressive north-east corrie of Stob Coire nan Lochan lies south-west of here. It gives some of the best winter climbs in Glencoe, but no worthwhile scrambles. Just below the lip of the corrie at G.R. 153 553, there is a slabby dome-shaped crag on which a short scramble can be made.

36. LOCHAN APPROACH   Grade 1/2

Scramble up the left edge, starting near the stream which flows from the lochans in the corrie above.

*   *   *

GEARR AONACH

The middle of the Three Sisters is known as Gearr Aonach *(short height)*. It has the shortest, but most impressive nose of all three. The idea of a scramble going up the left edge of the north face seems quite preposterous from the road, but that is just the line taken by one of the next two routes.

To the east of Gearr Aonach is the dramatic Coire Gabhail *(corrie of capture or booty)*, better known as the Lost Valley. The entrance to the corrie goes through a jumbled mass of gigantic boulders - debris from a huge landslide down the side of Gearr Aonach. The flat floor of the valley behind is most unexpected. It cannot be seen from the road, which is why it is sometimes known as the Hidden Valley. Stolen cattle are reputed to have been hidden there at one time. It is well worth a visit.

The two scrambles now described are both approached from the path up to the Lost Valley. Park as for the Aonach Eagach at G.R. 173 567, and cross the River Coe at a footbridge near the Meeting of Three Waters. The latter has been formed by erosion along two interesting dykes.

Follow the path up the hillside, and at a small outcrop take the higher, right-hand fork. Go up grassy slopes to a flatter area below the nose. The two routes play 'snakes and ladders' at the right-hand end of the north-east face.

37. THE ZIG-ZAGS   Grade 1   *

The 'snake'. This route barely warrants its grade. It is a useful descent route.

Ascend a narrow path up left to the contact between dark andesite and orange rhyolite. Follow the contact across right below some roofs. Then head up left again by a large step with some boulders. Continue easily up left and then walk back right and up to the crest of the ridge. Worth it for the views alone.

38. EASY ROUTE   Grade 3   **

The 'ladder'. Not as desperate as it looks. It does not fulfil its early promise, but it is a good scramble nevertheless. Low in the grade.

Take the first leg of the Zig-Zags along the andesite/rhyolite junction, then continue round the corner on the right for about 10m. The steep north face can be seen by going round a little further.

Step left onto a small heathery ledge and climb up the delightful rough rock. Go up some stepped recesses and reach a large sloping

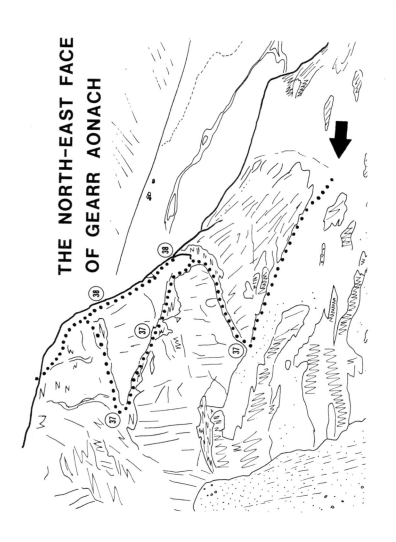

THE NORTH-EAST FACE OF GEARR AONACH

ledge below a steeper section.

Move up to a huge block and climb the crack on its left until able to step right. Continue up slightly left by a line which keeps as close as possible to the left edge. The rock is more lichenous now, but interest is maintained for some distance. The angle eases suddenly where the top section of the Zig-Zags is joined.

Take care when descending the Zig-Zags not to dislodge stones over the north-east face. It is a popular crag with climbers.

* * *

BEINN FHADA

The eastmost of the Three Sisters is called Beinn Fhada *(long mountain)*. It has the longest ridge of the three, but the least scrambling. The highest point on the ridge is the south-west top, which is called Stob Coire Sgreamhach *(peak of the dreadful corrie)*. This is also on the main ridge running down from Bidean nam Bian to Dalness in Glen Etive. The scramble now described is on a spur running off the ridge just mentioned, rather than on the flanks of Beinn Fhada itself.

39. SRON NA LAIRIG   Grade 2/3   **

The glen to the east of Beinn Fhada is called the Lairig Eilde *(pass of the hinds)*. Start from the main road, opposite a large cairn and follow a path for just over 3km all the way up the Lairig Eilde. Leave the path just before its high point and head up to the obvious ridge across on the right.

The scramble starts by ascending the edge on the top of a prominent slab at the foot of the ridge. Move up rock steps to begin with, then follow a short slab to the arête on the left. Ascend the crest of the ridge on good rock. At one point go up a groove in the crest, then follow the narrower ridge above. Eventually the ridge peters out on a grassy slope with boulders.

Directly above is too hard and unpleasant, so head hard right to a conspicuous slab. Surprisingly this proves to be rather difficult. Do not try to ascend it close up in the corner. Instead, start up a faint groove slightly lower down on the right. This is rather delicate, but the rock is excellent and the friction is good. When the groove disappears follow the rounded crest just right of the corner to the top. That is the hardest part over with.

Reach a small ribbon of scree and easier ground. Head up left-wards back to the centre of the ridge on indifferent, vegetated rock.

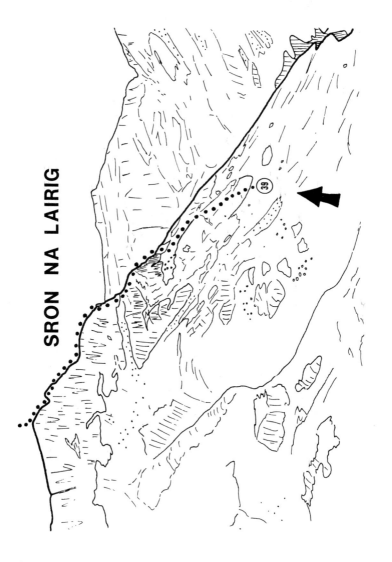

SRON NA LAIRIG

Arrive at a broad sloping terrace.

Go up to the centre of the rock band above, where there is a small, but obvious, triangular brown recess. Move up towards this, then go up right. Head diagonally leftwards for some distance, then slant right to a huge block forming a tower on the skyline. Clamber up blocks behind the tower and reach the easier ridge above.

The remainder of the ridge is narrow and twisting. It is quite exposed in places, but it is never difficult, (Grade 1). Two steeper sections are taken on the left by grassy steps. There are some enjoyable rock flakes on the arête in places.

From the summit, a pleasant circuit can be made by heading up to Stob Coire Sgreamhach, and then going down the Beinn Fhada ridge. There is a steep, rocky section just before the first col which is negotiated by twisting down to the right, (east) first, and then moving back left. There are no further difficulties on the rest of the ridge, but the end nose should be avoided by moving off to the right, and descending to the Lairig Eilde.

*   *   *

BUACHAILLE ETIVE BEAG

Across the Lairig Eilde from Beinn Fhada is another equally long mountain called Buachaille Etive Beag *(small herdsman of Etive)*. It has no scrambling to compare with its big brother to the east, except for one little gem on Creag nan Cabar *(crag of the antlers)* at the northern end of the mountain.

40. THE NORTH-EAST BUTTRESS OF CREAG NAN CABAR   Grade 2   **

Park near a bridge on the A82 at G.R. 192 562. Cross the road and head east-south-east for about 800m. Go past the main face of the crag to a tiny rock band below the left bounding buttress.

There is a grass ledge running from left to top right. Climb the left edge on good holds, then follow grass and scree to the buttress proper.

Zig-zag slightly all the way up the buttress never straying more than 6m from a grassy gully on the left. The rock is superb - rough and very sound.

Eventually the angle eases and the buttress fades out on a small terrace at a height of about 540m. The best scrambling is now over and a way down can be found by traversing west.

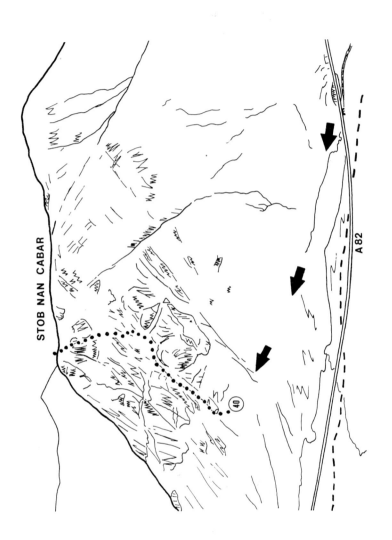

STOB NAN CABAR

A 82

40

Some short sections of rock can be picked out by continuing straight up the hillside. After a long grassy section, head up diagonally leftwards through the next area of rock. Reach a large slab and move across this leftwards. Step across a corner, then move up and back right. Continue to the summit of Stob nan Cabar. The highest top of Buachaille Etive Beag, Stob Dubh, is 3km away at the other end of the ridge.

* * *

BUACHAILLE ETIVE MOR

The mountain at the eastern end of Glencoe, called Buachaille Etive Mor, has the greatest concentration of quality scrambles of any mountain in the area. The sight of its huge conical mass, when driving north over Rannoch Moor, is enough to quicken the pulse of any dedicated scrambler, or climber.

Its main ridge is long and twisting, but most of the scrambling interest is at the north-east end, on the highest top called Stob Dearg *(red peak)*. This is more commonly referred to as simply 'The Buachaille'. North-west of the summit, there is a large corrie called Coire na Tulaich, which provides the easiest descent route from the mountain.

Two main approaches are used for scrambles on the Buachaille. The Jacksonville approach starts from a car park just off a bend in the road, north-east of the mountain, (G.R. 236 553). (There is rather an abrupt drop off the road, so mind the suspension.) It then goes over some stepping-stones, past a private shelter called Jacksonville, and straight up the hillside to a large slab of rock known as the Waterslide Slab.

The other approach starts from the north at a car park near Altnafeadh, (G.R. 220 563). It goes over the River Coupall by a footbridge, and then past the S.M.C. hut called Lagangarbh. The path splits shortly afterwards, one branch going up into Coire na Tulaich, and the other slanting left to join the Jacksonville path by the Waterslide Slab.

There are several major buttresses on the north side of the Buachaille. The broadest one, directly below the summit, is called North Buttress. To the left of this the mountain becomes rather more complex, and features can be difficult to identify, especially when close up under the face. However, the next buttress left of North Buttress can usually be picked out, because it has a prominent tower high up. This is the Crowberry Tower, on Crowberry Ridge.

Buachaille Etive Mor, Stob Dearg

The most important buttresses on the north face are shown in the diagram on page 96. The routes are described from right to left, the order in which they appear from Lagangarbh.

* * *

CREAG NA TULAICH

Just up in Coire na Tulaich from Lagangarbh, there is a three-tiered buttress called Creag na Tulaich. The next route starts from the path into the corrie, and goes up the crest of the buttress. Some rock climbing is to be had on the highest tier.

41. THE NORTH-EAST RIDGE OF
CREAG NA TULAICH   Grade 3   **

This delightful scramble is ideal for an evening's outing from Lagangarbh. Take the path up to Coire na Tulaich, and slant up right soon after crossing the Allt Coire na Tulaich. Reach the steep front wall of the first tier which is split by a crack. Avoid this by moving to the left, then start to move back right to the crest. A large slab appears on the left. Move up slightly and traverse delicately right to a more exposed position. Step up to easier angled slabs, and follow these to the second tier.

In the centre of the tier there is a vegetated recess with several small trees. Move up near the right-most tree, and go up a dyke on good holds trending right. Reach the crest of the buttress and follow easy stepped slabs to the third and largest tier.

Go up slabby rocks to a steeper section. This is too hard to climb direct, so go left round a corner to a ledge near a vegetated gully. The next section is one of the best parts of the route. Climb the steep wall immediately left of the corner on large holds. The rock is superb and the difficulties soon relent. The angle gradually eases to the top.

Descend the small col the other side of the summit. A pleasant way down traverses west from here to a slabby buttress which lies the other side of a broad grassy gully. It runs parallel to the line of ascent. A very steep crag lies further left.

The first major buttress to the east of Coire na Tulaich is called Lagangarbh Buttress. The lower part is broad and relatively easy, whilst the upper part is set back on the left and is of more interest to climbers. A gully slants up rightwards separating the upper buttress from the lower rocks.

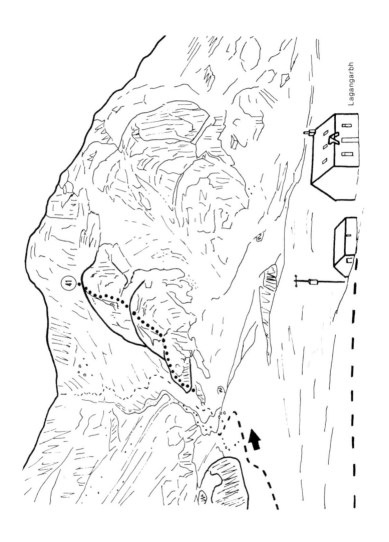

Lagangarbh

42. LAGANGARBH BUTTRESS   Grade 2/3   **

Although this scramble finishes fairly low down on the mountain, it does provide the most direct route to the·summit. The rock on the lower part is very good indeed.

Take the path from Lagangarbh and head up to the large mass of slabs at the bottom left of the buttress. Follow a narrow ribbon of slab up through heather to a shallow gully at the bottom right of the slabs. Move left across the gully and ascend slabby steps trending left. Continue for some distance on superb rough rock to a sloping heathery terrace.

Do not go up the steep rock above. Instead, follow an obvious ledge to the right. Then ascend an amazingly easy rock staircase back up left to another heather ledge. Move right again and follow a more difficult staircase through the next rock band. Trend up left-wards until it is possible to see a large gully some distance further left. The upper buttress is also visible at this point.

Now move back right and take the easiest line to a flatter section of the buttress. A wide wall, dripping with water, runs across the crest a little higher up. Go round to the right of this and stay on the right of the crest for some distance. Climbers will be able to find a way back to the crest up a short, steep wall.

Eventually reach more broken ground. Head up past a steep wall which appears on the left. This is the right wall of the upper buttress. Go up to a stepped corner at the top right-hand end of the wall. Ascend this by bridging on good holds. At the top, go up slightly, then traverse hard left across the top of the wall and so reach the crest of the upper buttress at a height of approximately 770m. It is easy from here to the summit of the Buachaille.

The west ridge from the summit leads down to the top of Coire na Tulaich. Turn right and drop down to the path which leads back to Lagangarbh.

43. BROAD BUTTRESS   Grade 2   **

Some distance left of Lagangarbh Buttress, there is a higher buttress called Broad Buttress. It is split by a groove high up, and bounded on the left by a trench-like grassy gully, called Narrow Gully.

Start at the apron of slabs at the bottom of the buttress. Find a way up these mainly in the centre, avoiding wet streaks as necessary. Reach easier ground and go up the much steeper rock above. Move round to the right and take a small easy gully back up to the centre of the buttress. Ascend just left of a faint groove and weave up until

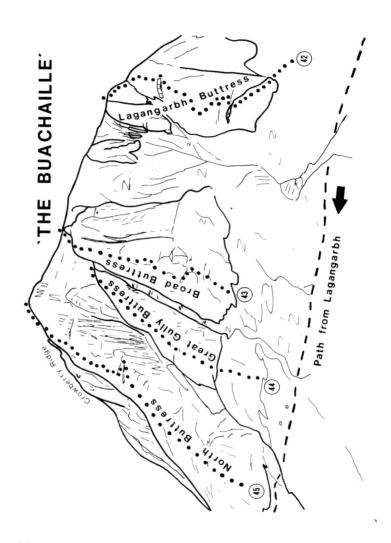

'THE BUACHAILLE'

Lagangarbh Buttress

Broad Buttress

Great Gully Buttress

North Buttress

Crowberry Ridge

Path from Lagangarbh

42

43

44

45

another large rock band is reached.

Head for the top right-hand side, and follow a line of steps leading up right for a short distance. Move back up left at a slabby scoop. Pass to the right of a boulder and ascend a pleasant slab.

Continue for some distance on delightful rough rock - the best part of the scramble - and eventually reach the top. Go over another minor bump and join a path on scree which curves round left to the summit.

44. GREAT GULLY BUTTRESS   Grade 1/2   *

The buttress immediately left of Broad Buttress is known as Great Gully Buttress. It is separated from Broad Buttress by the trench-like gully already mentioned, and bounded on the left by the Great Gully itself. It gives a rather vegetated route, but good fun can be had on some of the cleaner rock slabs. Much variation is possible, but generally a central position on the buttress should be maintained.

A steeper section early on is best ascended at the left-hand side. Some distance higher, just above a ledge with a large boulder, a slabby rock band is climbed by a groove in the centre.

The best rock band is towards the top. At its base on the right-hand side, there is a steep wall. Start at the left-hand end of the wall and follow a line up the centre of some delightful slabs. Zig-zag slightly towards the top.

Eventually emerge at the top of the buttress. There is a large rock wall across on the right. This is the top left-hand side of Broad Buttress, although it is known to climbers as Great Gully Upper Buttress. Move past this and curve round right to reach the top of Broad Buttress. Finish as for that route.

45. NORTH BUTTRESS   Grade 3   *

The huge buttress directly below the summit is called North Buttress. On its right-hand side a very intimidating rock wall, the Slime Wall, rises out of Great Gully.

With good route finding this scramble will be found easy for its grade. The lower half is little more than a walk. The situation is good, but in the central section the rock is not up to the Buachaille's usual standard. It improves towards the top.

The buttress is easily recognised by two large boulders on a slight shoulder not far above the path from Lagangarbh. Take almost any line on the lower section, ascending heathery ledges, scree and occasional rock steps. Start to move slightly right after a while - good views of Great Gully Buttress.

At a major steepening of the buttress, reach an obvious narrow ledge and path which leads horizontally left below the rock face. Follow this to a prominent crack/chimney line in the centre of the buttress. Ascend the crack for a short section, and then avoid its continuation by taking an obvious break on the right. Move up and round to the right then head back up left to the centre of the buttress and easy ledges.

Another crack/chimney line can be seen higher up. Make for this up a rightward slanting groove. Ascend in the left part of the chimney at first, then step up right to a small ledge made of jammed blocks. Now ascend the right-hand section of chimney for a short distance. Higher up the chimneys merge and peter out to a crack. Avoid this by stepping out right and following an easy gangway rightwards.

Step up left and follow more solid slabby rock straight up on good holds. More good scrambling continues for some distance. The angle eases all the way to the summit. There are good views of the Crowberry Tower on the left, near the top, as well as Rannoch Moor stretching away in the distance.

The next two scrambles are best seen from the Jacksonville direction, although they can still be approached from Lagangarbh. The gully left of North Buttress is known as Crowberry Gully. Left of this is Crowberry Ridge with its prominent tower. Sweeping up below the base of Crowberry Ridge, and joining on to the side of it below Crowberry Tower, is the Curved Ridge.

These two ridges are separated by Easy Gully. On the left side of Crowberry Ridge above Easy Gully, there is a spectacular rock wall, the Rannoch Wall, which has some classic rock climbs. Agag's Groove is a delightful Very Difficult grade climb in a stupendous situation. Details of this and many other excellent climbs can be found in 'Glencoe and Glen Etive (Rock and Ice Climbs)' by K.V. Crocket and published by the Scottish Mountaineering Trust.

Both scrambles are reached by zig-zagging up loose soil and scree to the left of the Waterslide Slab. Head well over to the right, back to near the water again. Then move up left slightly on worn rocks, and continue some distance to a point overlooking the junction between Easy Gully and Crowberry Gully. A steep rock rib is directly above. This is the start of Curved Ridge proper. In Easy Gully on the right, there is a similar parallel rock rib.

BUACHAILLE
ETIVE MOR

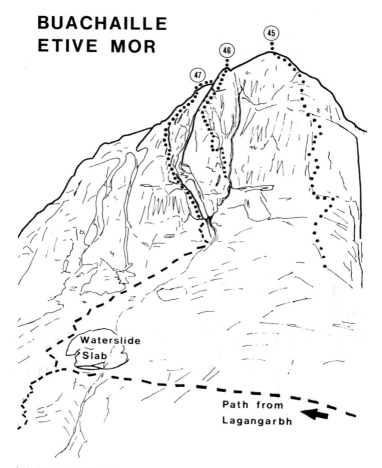

46. CROWBERRY RIDGE   Grade 3(S)   ***

Many variations have been worked out on the lower half of
Crowberry Ridge. This combination starts up the original line
pioneered by Naismith in 1896, and then traverses left onto the
exposed crest of the ridge and follows this to the top. It therefore
avoids the problematical direct start, but still samples the superb
situation on the main part of the ridge. Even so, it is a serious

undertaking and only suitable for those able to cope with difficulties in exposed situations. It is probably the hardest route in this guide.

From the junction of Easy Gully and Crowberry Gully, go across right and up to a broad terrace below the east face of North Buttress. This point can also be reached from the front of North Buttress. There is a good view of the lower part of the route from here.

Go up the bed of Crowberry Gully until a cave is reached with mossy walls. Traverse out along the left wall, and move round to grassy ledges. An alternative start from Easy Gully comes in from the left at this point.

There are three chimney lines above. Move up to the left-most one. This was ascended by Naismith on the original ascent, but it is rather difficult. So step across right into the central chimney. Make a mantelshelf move to gain a ledge on the right. Continue up the rib above to easier ground. (This is the start of Shelf Route.)

Head up left some distance towards the obvious gully of Naismith's Route. Just short of this, traverse a prominent ledge which runs out across the left wall. It becomes more difficult at the end, but the holds are good. Stay low and move round on to the front of the ridge. The exposure is considerable here.

Continue left to the centre of the ridge on an easy ledge, (called Upper Ledge). Ascend the obvious groove straight up on good holds. Reach another ledge and a good belay.

Make an awkward step up into a small recess, then move up a short distance until the rock starts to bulge above. With careful foot-work a good handhold can be reached by a delicate move right. Now ascend more easily to a big ledge on the right side of the ridge.

Move left to the crest and go up this in a magnificent position. The rock is excellent, and there are plenty of holds. One or two high step-ups add a little interest. The angle eases and the main difficulties are now over.

Continue easily up the crest of the ridge, with steep drops down Rannoch Wall on the left. Just above a large rightward slanting glacis, step up right instead of moving left on a narrow path. Maintain position on the ridge crest and finish up the north side of Crowberry Tower.

From the summit of the tower go back down the north side for a short distance. Now either spiral round to the left and so reach the col on the west side of the tower, or go down the north ridge a little further and traverse back across the east face to the top of Curved Ridge.

100

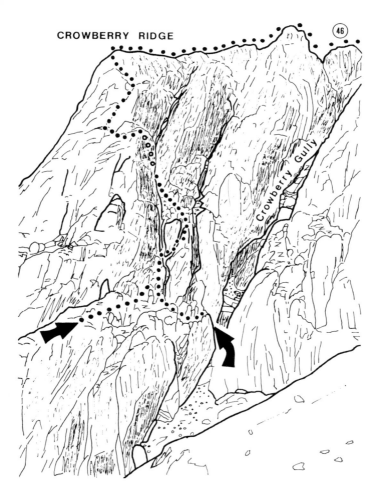

It is not far from the col on the west side of the tower to the summit of the Buachaille. Alternatively, those who have had no difficulties on Crowberry Ridge, may prefer to descend Curved Ridge.

47. CURVED RIDGE   Grade 2/3   **

This route gets its stars for situation, rather than for the quality of the actual scrambling. It gives unrivalled views of Rannoch Wall on the right and the vast expanse of Rannoch Moor on the left. The rock climbing routes on Rannoch Wall look especially breathtaking from this angle. It is a very popular route.

Reach the junction of Easy Gully and Crowberry Gully as described above. Head up the obvious rock rib beside Easy Gully. The whole route is very well worn and no route finding problems should be encountered from here on. Continue up a more jagged crest above, trending slightly left.

After a long easy section on a stony path reach another steep section with a gully and rock rib on the right-hand side of it. Stay out of the gully and go up the rock on the left. Ascend a rightward slanting groove on good holds to a platform. Continue up a series of large rock ledges on well worn holds.

The ridge becomes more broken, with one or two awkward steps. It finishes at a cairn below Crowberry Tower. Go rightwards below the east face of the tower and join the north ridge which leads easily to its summit.

Return down the north ridge a short distance, then spiral down to the left and drop into the col on the west side of the tower. Scramble up the other side for some distance, then continue easily to the summit of the Buachaille.

The last scramble described on the Buachaille follows a long rising traverse line on the south-east face. The shortest approach starts from the Glen Etive road.

48. THE CHASM TO CROWBERRY TRAVERSE
Grade 3(S)

Although this route follows a natural traverse line, there is something unsatisfactory about it. Long parts of it are easy, but the main difficulties are unreasonable even though they are short. The crucial section is on suspect rock and in a somewhat claustrophobic situation. However, there are some better moments!

Two major gullies slice into the left-hand half of the south-east face. The longer right-hand one is known as The Chasm. The scramble starts from the right-hand bank of The Chasm and traverses a long way up to the right, eventually finishing near the Crowberry Tower.

Park just over 2km down the Glen Etive road. Head across to The Chasm and follow a faint path up the right (north) bank. (G.R. 228 537). At the first rock band follow a zig-zag line starting from the left on superb holds.

Continue easily to a large rock wall. The Chasm North Wall rock climb carries on up from here. Instead, follow a delightful diagonal line leading to the right. This finishes at a narrow scree gully. Move right, then back left and go up the loose scree for some distance, all the time slanting to the right.

Pass below a large slanting roof, and when the way on looks rather steep, move out right and go round a corner. A large gully comes up from the right at this point, (the left fork of Lady's Gully). Cross the top of the gully, and climb up some rather smooth rocks, which are wet in places.

Reach an enclosed section of more shattered rock. The wet groove on the left is much harder than it looks. Stay well to the right of it and ascend a rounded broken rib. This is the crux, and it is sustained for nearly 15m. The holds are not as reassuring as one would like.

Move up a shallow recess slightly right, to a more open position with good views. Move up leftwards, then head more or less straight up for some distance. Trend across right until the top of Curved Ridge comes into view (cairn), with Crowberry Tower above. All this last section is on fairly loose ground, although easy technically.

Either go up scree to the col on the west side of the tower and continue to the summit of the Buachaille, or descend Curved Ridge. The south shoulder gives a convenient descent to Glen Etive from the summit.

*   *   *

The Etive Hills

Glen Etive is one of the most beautiful glens in the area. A single-track road leaves the A82 not far west of the Kingshouse Hotel, and runs for 23km down the glen, before coming to a dead-end by the head of Loch Etive. There are many fine hills bordering the glen, but surprisingly few which offer any scrambling.

At the top end of Glen Ceitlein, which runs off Glen Etive, there are some remarkably long but easy slabs in Coirean Riabhach. These enliven an ascent of the north-north-west side of Meall Tarsuinn. After starting up a stream bed, almost any line can be followed.

Ben Starav is a magnificent granite mountain on the east side of Loch Etive, but only its east ridge running out to Stob Coire Dheirg gives any scrambling of note. The short section of easy Grade 1 arête is normally included in a traverse of the peak.

On the west side of Loch Etive, opposite Ben Starav, is another granite mountain called Beinn Trilleachan. On its eastern flank there are some immense slabs, the Etive Slabs, which give a unique type of climbing in this country. The slabs are set at a critical angle which makes it just possible to climb them by relying solely upon friction, rather than by using definite holds. The climbs are all fairly hard, and there are no scrambling possibilities here.

Over on the other side of the north-north-east ridge some similar slabs are set at a more reasonable angle. The route now described gives a taste of friction scrambling! It should only be attempted in dry weather.

49. COIRE CRICHE SLAB ROUTE   Grade 3(S)   **

Leave the Glen Etive road on the west side of a fence bounding a huge plantation, (G.R. 110 453). This is only 500m from the end of the road. Head up the hillside not far from the fence, and eventually pick up a rather wet path which goes around the end of the north-north-east ridge of the mountain.

When the fence makes an abrupt turn to the right, head south-west along the Allt Criche. (The path continues over to Glen Ure.) Reach some slightly flatter ground with good views of the slabby hillside above Coire Criche *(end corrie)*. Head south and then south-east to the most continuous stretch of slabs, just to the left of a broad vegetated gully.

Join the main slab from the right and go up it easily at first.

104

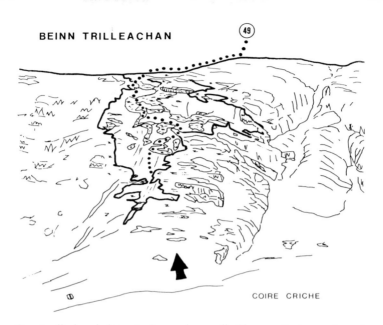

COIRE CRICHE

Eventually hands have to be used as well. The granite is rough and sound. Pull over a small overlap using handfuls of heather. Go up grass to a very short section of slab. Climb this and continue on grass again.

Traverse right across a rock slab at an obvious weakness. Continue up slightly right on vegetation, then follow a leftward-leaning groove. Reach a crevice containing a very small rowan tree.

The big slabs straight above are too hard, so start to traverse left. Then go up slabby rock, until it is possible to traverse further left. Care is needed here, because the rock is wet in places. Then go up vegetation and ascend a rock flake near its top right corner.

Go left and up to a prominent slab with a large boulder resting on it. Ascend the slab passing to the right of the boulder. This is rather delicate, but not as bad as it looks. The hardest part is about half way up.

At the top, go up a narrow rib of vegetation, then step left onto a foothold. Make a delicate step up onto a higher section of slab, using fingerholds in a narrow horizontal crack. Follow the delightful

105

tapering slab to easier ground.

Romp up a long easy slab to more grassy terrain interspersed with numerous short slabs. String together the slabs until a short, steep rock step is reached. Climb this at a recess formed by a large fallen block. This gives a few pleasant pull-ups on good holds.

Reach the crest of the north-north-east ridge, and follow easy angled granite slabs, with fine views, to a top at 767m. The famous Etive Slabs are directly below, although they cannot be seen from here. Very few climbers come up this far for the view.

The summit of Beinn Trilleachan is still about 1300m away, but the quickest descent from here is down a grassy gully on the left, at the next col on the ridge, (693m). This becomes rather bouldery towards the bottom. When the gully becomes more open, some distance above a wood, start moving round to the left. Then head hard over to the left, staying below the gigantic slabs (the Etive Slabs), but above the woods.

Move up slightly to stay above the trees, and eventually reach a large flat slab, called the Coffin Stone, which lies at the base of the Etive Slabs towards the right-hand side. Climbers congregate here, before and after doing routes on the slabs.

Follow a path from the Coffin Stone all the way back to the end of the Glen Etive road. There is an awkward rock step at about the 200m contour.

*   *   *

Creise - Stob A'Ghlais Choire on the left (Route 51)
Sron Na Creise on the right (Route 50)

The Blackmount

The superb group of hills on the west side of the A82, between the Glen Etive turn-off and Bridge of Orchy, is known as the Blackmount. There is a real feeling of remoteness in the centre of the range around Coireach a' Ba, which is accentuated by the great expanse of Rannoch Moor to the east. The next few scrambles however, are reasonably accessible, being on mountains at the northern and southern extremities of the group.

CREISE

This mountain lies on the opposite side of Glen Etive from Buachaille Etive Mor. There are good views of its northern end from the Kingshouse Hotel. At the southern end of the mountain is the former Munro called Clach Leathad, which at 1098m is now deemed to be 2 metres lower than Creise.

The next two scrambles are both on the northern top called Stob a' Ghlais Choire *(peak of the grey corrie)*. In low water conditions they can be approached from Glen Etive, but otherwise the more usual start is from the vicinity of Blackrock Cottage.

50. SRON NA CREISE   Grade 3   **

The north ridge of Stob a' Ghlais Choire is called Sron na Creise. It is possible to ascend most of the shoulder without any scrambling at all. Conversely, by deliberately hunting out the best rock outcrops a really magnificent scramble can be pieced together. It is low in the grade.

Either hop across boulders in the River Etive or skirt around Creag Dhubh from Blackrock Cottage. The lower part of the shoulder is a grassy plod with minor outcrops. Go up the centre of the first significant rock step where it is lighter in colour. It is steep towards the top, but the holds are excellent.

Keep heading slightly left from here and after some distance reach a point level with a gigantic boulder on the left. The fun starts on a prominent slabby buttress above and left of the boulder.

Start at a leftward-slanting, narrow grassy groove. The first few moves up this are steep and awkward, but it soon eases. Continue to the crest of the buttress, and arrive at the base of delightful slabs. Go up these to a small recess, which is exited by a step left. Carry on up until a second, rather bigger buttress comes up from the left.

Go across to this and ascend a short groove. Make a difficult move to get established on top of a block. Then pull up onto the wall above and soon reach very good holds. Follow these trending left, until it becomes easy to move up to a ledge with loose stones. Continue more easily.

Ascend a rightward leaning groove with a vertical left wall, then move left and follow a slab to easy ground. It is now possible to look into a gully on the right. Stay on this side of the gully for some distance. Eventually traverse right across the gully and reach another buttress on the other side. It is important to find the correct level here, so as to avoid the steep lower section of the right-hand buttress.

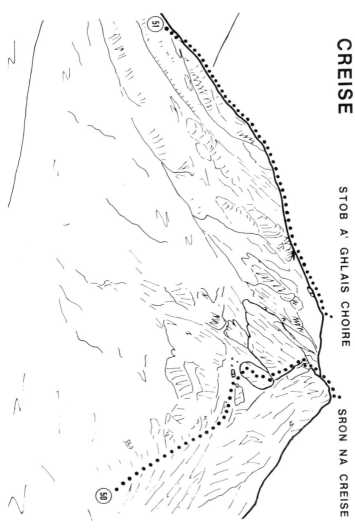

CREISE

STOB A' GHLAIS CHOIRE

SRON NA CREISE

109

From a small ledge make a step out to the right, and move round onto the right-hand side of the buttress. Follow superb holds all the way up. Move up to the last buttress, which has a steep step up to start, and then follow the crest to easy ground and the top of the Sron. It is easy from here to the summit of Stob a' Ghlais Choire.

A good circuit can be made by continuing over the summit of Creise, and going out along the arête to Meall a' Bhuiridh. Descend the broad north ridge, with ski-tows on the right. Those returning to Blackrock Cottage sometimes have the option of descending the last section from the plateau by chairlift - the only artificial aid of its type in the area.

51. NORTH-EAST RIDGE OF STOB A' GHLAIS CHOIRE
Grade 1 or 2   **

Approach as for the previous route. Leave the Allt Cam Ghlinne just below a waterfall, and head up the broad grassy hillside, with occasional rock slabs. Arrive at a slight flattening at a height of about 540m. Another section of grass slope leads to the start of the ridge proper.

Follow an easy ramp up right. There are various possibilities from here, but the most pleasant is to traverse left along an obvious terrace, and then move up easily to the right. Continue up to the right until the angle eases and another mass of rock appears above.

Move left to get established on this and ascend it on large holds. A short scree slope develops on the right near the top. There is a grassy band above, with an obvious section of slabby rock on its left. Reach the slab and go up maintaining the same line to the next steep slabby section.

The Grade 2 option continues the same direct line by finding a way up a small recess with a crack above. The easier option moves rightwards to where the rock is more accommodating. A long stretch of enjoyable rough rock follows.

Eventually the buttress peters out on a terrace at 870m. A scree slope leads from here to the summit. Go over Creise as for the previous route. Care is needed, in poor visibility, to find the descent for Meall a' Bhuiridh.

The next outing is reached by turning off the main road at Bridge of Orchy and following a single track road to Victoria Bridge. From here a track goes west to the tiny Clashgour Hut at G.R. 256.424, run by Glasgow University M.C. A very good stalker's path then goes north beside the Allt Toaig, and gives remarkably easy access to the impressive Stob Ghabhar and another Munro called Stob a' Choire Odhair.

*   *   *

STOB GHABHAR

Many different ridges and tops lead to the summit of Stob Ghabhar *(peak of the goats)*. The east-south-east ridge is called the Aonach Eagach. Whilst nowhere as good as its namesake in Glencoe, it does have some entertainment to offer the scrambler.

52. THE SOUTH-EAST NOSE OF THE AONACH
EAGACH   Grade 3   *

Follow the stalker's path beside the Allt Toaig as far as the confluence with the Allt Coire na Muic, (G.R. 251 439). Cross the Allt Toaig and go up beside a wire fence to a prominent waterfall *(An Steallair)*. In dry conditions this gives a most enjoyable Grade 2 ** scramble, which is not described.

Cross over the stream and ascend a short leftward slanting groove. Go up some distance, then move right and step over the water again. Climb a steep wall on good holds by moving to and fro. When the angle starts to ease move over to the right near the wire fence. Then ascend one last pleasant section to the final rock wall. This has to be avoided by moving right, up the grassy hillside. In high water conditions the whole waterfall is avoided on the right.

Head north across undulating, boggy ground to the start of the Aonach Eagach. The bottom section is better and easier than it looks.

Go up scree to a rock rib. Move across to the right-hand side of the steep bottom part. Go up at first, then move left onto the crest of the rib. Continue more easily, but still with some interest, to a steeper mass of rock.

The first 3m up this are the hardest, (they can be turned on the left if required). Break up through the formidable section of rock above by a vague recess with good holds. Emerge on easier ground. Go up some distance, then traverse left to a large area of pink slabby rock.

Ascend the centre of an easy angled slab, criss-crossed with cracks. At the top of this, it is possible to move left into a large recess with further easy slabs. Instead, make an awkward step or two right, and gain the bottom of a prominent crack. Climb same on surprisingly good holds. The exposure becomes noticeable here. Continue on

111

very good rock with a difficult step up left at one point. This whole section is fairly sustained, and constitutes the crux of the route.

Reach a grassy terrace and move slightly right to further rock. Go up this to more broken ground on the broad crest of the ridge.

Head up the ridge for 1km. Just when it starts to become tedious it levels out and narrows to an arête. There are fine views of the summit cliffs and the corrie below. The narrow section of ridge is exhilarating, but not difficult. It is easy then to the summit of Stob Ghabhar.

An enjoyable circuit can be made by traversing over the summit, and following the ridge around Coirein Lochain towards Sron nan Giubhas. Some way down the ridge, at G.R. 242 464, turn back rightwards and slant down into the corrie along the Aisre nan Each *(path of the horses)*.

Contour round the lip separating the upper corrie, Coirein Lochain, from the lower corrie, Coire Dhearbhadh. Make a rising traverse to the south-east and so gain the bealach at the head of Coire Toaig. Continue heading south-east down the corrie and eventually pick up the stalker's path which leads back to the starting point. Or pop up Stob a' Choire Odhair on the way.

*　　*　　*

Ben Cruachan

One of the best ridge walks in the area is a traverse of the long and mighty Ben Cruachan, the most southerly mountain in this guide. Its name should more properly be given as Cruachan Beann, which means mountain of peaks. It has eight main summits, but few of them are named on O.S. maps. They are, from west to east, Stob Dearg (1104m), Ben Cruachan (1126m), Drochaid Ghlas (1009m), Stob Diamh (998m), and Sron an Isean (966m). The remaining summits are on spurs running south off the main ridge; Meall Cuanail (918m) south of Ben Cruachan, Stob Garbh (980m) and Beinn a' Bhuiridh (896m) both south of Stob Diamh.

The scrambles now described are not particularly inspiring, but since they are at opposite ends of the mountain they can be used to start a traverse from either direction.

* * *

53. EAST RIDGE OF STOB GARBH   Grade 1

The eastern end of the Ben Cruachan can be approached along either of two good tracks which are not marked on the O.S. 1:50,000 map. The scramble is reached from the one leading to some old lead mines on the north-east flank of Monadh Driseig. The track starts from the western end of the B8077 loop road (G.R. 132 283), and goes north and then west. Take the left fork past the mouth of a quarry and continue along the remains of a railway to a good bridge over the Allt Coire Ghlais. Cross the bridge and head up into Coire Chreachainn. There is no path to speak of, but after an initial boggy section the going becomes easy enough.

Reach a waterfall where the Allt Coire Chreachainn flows over a large step of granite. The east ridge of Stob Garbh *(rugged peak)* rises due west of here.

Head up to the right-hand side of the ridge to avoid the steep and unattractive bottom section. Cut back left to the crest of the ridge and follow this, mainly on grass with some minor outcrops and boulders.

The ridge pinches down where a gully runs up from the south face. Above, the ground becomes steeper, but it stays grassy and is never difficult. At a block split by a kinked crack, it is necessary to move right and pass another higher block on the right, before moving back left to the crest. The ridge broadens again.

113

Higher up the ridge narrows, twists and turns, before finishing close to the summit. A simple horseshoe can be made by returning over either Sron an Isean, or Beinn a' Bhuiridh, but most people will continue to Ben Cruachan.

Returning from the summit, a different way back can be taken by descending the north ridge of Drochaid Ghlas *(grey bridge)*, then heading north-east to a track on the west side of the Lairig Noe. Leave the track and climb up over the bealach at 564m, (some marker posts in places). Drop down the other side to a good track which leads back to the B 8077, about half a kilometre north-east of the starting place.

54. THE NORTH RIDGE OF STOB DEARG   Grade 1   *

Stob Dearg *(red peak)* is at the western end of the range, and is often referred to as the Taynuilt Peak. Its north ridge is rather difficult to approach. It can be reached by ascending the Allt Cruiniche from the A85 near Bridge of Awe, and then descending the bealach between Stob Dearg and Meall nan Each. The approach from the remote Glen Noe on the north side of the mountain involves a much longer walk. Either take the old military road from Bridge of Awe, and with permission continue on a very rough track to Glennoe Farm, or follow the track from the B 8077 on the east side of the Allt Mhoille and go over the Lairig Noe. The latter alternative is more practical if a traverse of the mountain is intended, although it does entail a descent of more than 200m from the Lairig Noe.

On the north-west side of the peak there are some large granite slabs. Those descending from the bealach between Stob Dearg and Meall nan Each can traverse the bottom of them to reach the north ridge.

Head up the crest of the ridge, close to Coire Chat on the left. Follow any number of granite slabs interspersed with grassy ledges. Much variation is possible. Higher up, the ridge is covered by gigantic slabby flakes and blocks of rough, pink granite. Squeeze up between these, keeping as close as possible to the crest of the ridge. Finish right on the summit.

*   *   *

One of the largest pumped storage schemes in the world has been built in the heart of Ben Cruachan. The road, dam and reservoir on the south side of the mountain are the only external signs of a huge underground complex. There is a visitors' centre at the Falls of Cruachan, which might be of interest on a wet day.

The Glen Creran Hills

Where the road between Glencoe and Oban loops around the head of Loch Creran, a side-road leads off up Glen Creran. This gives access to Glen Ure and two Munros called Beinn Sgulaird and Beinn Fhionnlaidh. There are granite slabs in Coire nan Capull on the west side of Beinn Sgulaird which give quite good climbing when they dry out. The best scrambling, however, is on the south face of Beinn Fhionnlaidh.

* * *

55. SOUTH FACE OF BEINN FHIONNLAIDH
Grade 2 *

Park in Glen Creran near Elleric at G.R. 036 488, and walk along to Glenure House. There are two options from here. Either turn left, go along to a wood and then find a path which leads up to Lochan na h-Uraich, or turn right, cross a bridge over the River Ure and follow first a track and then a path, until it it possible to recross the river. Head north-east over Meall nam Fiadh (438m), and continue in the same direction, then cross two streams due north of Lochan na Fola. The second route is longer, but gives better views of the face.

There is much scrambling on this side of Beinn Fhionnlaid *(Finlay's mountain)*. The route described takes a line parallel to, but just higher than, a narrow intrusion of pink coloured rock which slants up the face from left to right.

Go up the right (east) bank of a large gully with a waterfall, the Eas nan Clach Reamhar *(waterfall of the large boulders)*. Start trending right up a series of short easy steps of mica schist. A much smaller gully develops on the left.

The best section starts at some steeper rocks just left of the pink rock band. Weave to and fro following the line of least resistance. There are several short rock walls with good holds. The rocks start to lie back and an obvious section of shattered quartz vein leads to easy ground.

Continue in the same direction and cross some scree to a small rock buttress. Climb the left-hand side, with a slimy moss streak further right. Keep slanting up right over large boulders, then head straight up to another section of rock. Go up pleasantly to a 3m wall with thin quartz veins slanting up it from left to right. Surprisingly this can be ascended by a traverse line which finishes at the top right-

115

BEINN FHIONNLAIDH

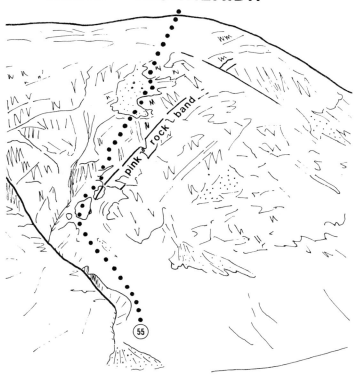

hand corner.

The scrambling now peters out and any line can be followed up right for some distance to the summit. Either descend the west ridge, or go along the east ridge, and descend by a fence, down rocky steps, to Bealach Caol Creran, before returning along Glen Creran.

* * *

The Appin Hills

The region from Glen Creran to Loch Leven, known as Appin, is dominated by the huge horseshoe of Beinn a' Bheithir *(mountain of the monster or thunderbolt),* which lies just south of the Ballachulish Bridge. Two scenic scrambles are described from here, one inside and one outside the horseshoe.

Although the mountain is called Beinn a' Bheithir (pronounced Vair), none of its three main summits take that name. The highest peak is called Sgorr Dhearg (1024m), the next is Sgorr Dhonuill (1001m), and un-named on O.S. maps is Sgorr Bhan (947m).

Gleann a' Chaolais *(glen of the strait)* forms the inside of the horseshoe. Unfortunately some very dense afforestation has made the top end of the glen almost inaccessible. Whoever organised the planting here gave little consideration to hillgoers wishing to reach the northern slopes of Sgorr Dhonuill. This is a pity, because jutting north from Sgorr Dhonuill there is a prominent spur called Sgorr a' Chaolais which gives a fine scramble.

56. THE TRAVERSE OF SGORR A' CHAOLAIS
Grade 2   **

The O.S. 1:25,000 map (Glencoe) is invaluable for reaching and descending from this scramble. Some 800m west of the Ballachulish Bridge, take a small turning to Glenachulish. Park after 750m and take a forestry track heading south. Some distance along this, turn left over the stream and continue south on the other side of the glen. Go round two hairpin bends and reach a crossroads at G.R. 044 569. Turn left and after 350m pass the foundations of a small building. 75m further on a small path leads off on the right by a stream.

The path becomes difficult to follow. Cross two tiny streams, heading more or less in a southeasterly direction. Eventually reach a gap in a wire fence. Go through this and move right to a more open area. Cross a stream and then follow a continuation of the path (several small cairns) up beside a stream-bed, heading south and then south-east. Cross a new fence (unmarked on O.S. map) at a small stile, and continue up to an old wire deer-fence. Head right (south-west) along this until it changes direction, then cut across the floor of the glen and up the other side, until it is possible to traverse round to the north side of Sgorr a' Chaolais.

117

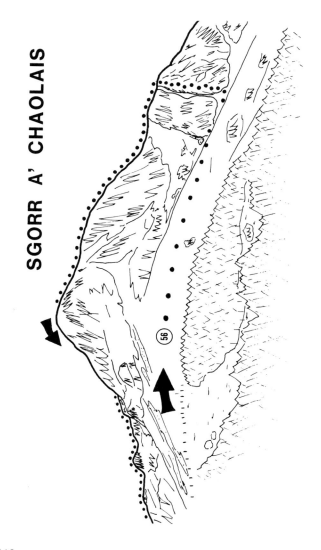

SGORR A' CHAOLAIS

Sgorr A'Chaolais (Route 56)

There are some rocky ribs on the opposite side of a large grassy bay. Follow a prominent sheep track across to the second rib from the left. There is a narrow grassy gully on its left. This east facing rib is rather vegetated, and the rock is suspect in places, but with care it gives an interesting ascent. Weave to and fro up heathery rock steps, some of them quite steep. It remains fairly narrow and requires concentration, until it finishes suddenly at a slight shoulder on the hillside. That is the crux over with.

A long plod up grassy terrain leads to some small, slabby outcrops of granite. Boulders become more numerous towards the top of the Sgorr. There are fine views from here.

An undulating arête connects the flat summit of the Sgorr to the east ridge of Sgorr Dhonuill *(Donald's Peak)*. The first part of the ridge is easy, but then it starts to demand some attention. The first difficulty is descending a short section of flaky rock. The rather bigger drop from the next small top is much harder. It is best negotiated by moving down the left-hand side and facing in at times.

Continue more easily, moving over and round granite blocks, until the main ridge is reached. The summit of Sgorr Dhonuill is not far above.

119

The west ridge can be descended, but the forest below Coire Dearg is hard going. The best way back is over Sgorr Dhearg and down its long north ridge to the Allt na Leachd. This leads to a track which curves west and south-west back to Gleann a' Chaolais.

57. THE EAST-NORTH-EAST RIDGE
OF SGORR BHAN   Grade 1   *

Sgorr Bhan *(white peak)* is linked by a beautiful curving ridge to Sgorr Dhearg *(red peak)*. The summit of the latter is made of quartzite, but it probably gets its name from the red granite on its north ridge and western flank.

This scramble is very straightforward and gives magnificent views of Loch Leven and the surrounding hills. It is low in the grade.

Turn off the main road and enter Ballachulish village (East and West Laroch). Find a road which runs along the west bank of the River Laroch, sign-posted 'Public Footpath to Glen Creran'. Park in the village and walk along this road to a farm. Continue along a track as far as a locked gate, then head up to the obvious ridge on the right.

After a long grassy section, small rock outcrops start to appear, and a path develops as the ridge gets narrower. The rock strata run across the ridge and the small outcrops are broken into little ledges. The rock is rather shattered and has to be treated carefully. It consists of quartzite with thin intercalations of slate. The rusty brown colouration is due to weathering of abundant iron minerals.

Towards the top, the rock changes to whiter quartzite without the slate, and it also becomes slightly sounder. The scrambling ends at the junction with the north-north-east ridge. Continue easily to the summit of Sgorr Bhan.

From the col the other side of the summit, a quick descent can be made back to the Glen Creran path by heading south-east and then east to a shoulder above the Allt Sheileach.

*   *   *

There is a ravine on the south-west flank of Beinn a' Bheithir called Eas nam Meirleach *(waterfall of the thieves)*. It is spectacular feature which is worth making a detour from the west ridge of Sgorr Dhonuill to have a look at from above. Despite being described as a scramble elsewhere, it is mainly an unpleasant trudge up boulders. It is not recommended.

*   *   *

Garbh Bheinn - Pinnacle Ridge (Route 58)

THE WESTERN GROUP

The Western Group is bounded to the east by Loch Linnhe, and to the north by Loch Eil and the road to Lochailort. It is a very picturesque region of varied character. Two long narrow lochs, one saltwater (Loch Sunart), and one freshwater (Loch Shiel), cut deeply into the area. The district to the west of Loch Shiel is known as Moidart, and there is some very fine hillwalking there. However, the highest and most rugged hills occur to the east of Loch Shiel in a district known as Ardgour.

Ardgour

The most striking mountain of the district, called Garbh Bheinn, is actually the second highest. It is easily the most popular with walkers and climbers. The shortest route to Ardgour is via the Corran ferry across Loch Linnhe, but there is also a road around the head of Loch Eil.

*   *   *

GARBH BHEINN

Although not a Munro, Garbh Bheinn *(rough mountain)* has a finer form than many mountains of that status. Its bold rock ridges and buttresses make an impressive sight even when seen at a distance from the Corran ferry. The rock is a rough, grey gneiss with some lesser amounts of quartzite. It is superb for climbing.

Park a short distance up Glen Tarbert on a section of old road at the foot of Coire an Iubhair, (10km from Corran). Follow a path up the east bank of the Abhainn Coire an Iubhair for more than 3km. It is quite wet in places.

58. PINNACLE RIDGE   Grade 3 (S)   ***

Turn up left by the Allt a' Gharbh Choire Mhoir. Pinnacle Ridge is the long stepped ridge which sweeps up from the right side of the stream. The bottom part is straightforward, but the main pinnacle, which is in fact just a steepening of the ridge, is quite serious and sustained. The remaining section of ridge is no more than Grade 2, and very enjoyable.

Some distance up the path by the Allt a' Gharbh Choire Mhoir, there is a small overhung rock wall on the right. Just after this, and just before reaching a prominent tree by the stream, head right up steep grass to gain the broad toe of the ridge.

Any number of rock outcrops can be ascended from here. The rock is excellent and holds abundant. After a very minor top, descend to a col with a tiny lochan. Continue by a choice of lines on good rock. The angle then eases again and boulders become more common.

Approach the steep crucial buttress by first climbing a short rock rib trending slightly left on knobbly holds. In the centre of the buttress, there is an obvious recess with a clean-cut back wall, capped by a sloping roof. Move well to the left of this, then go up and right

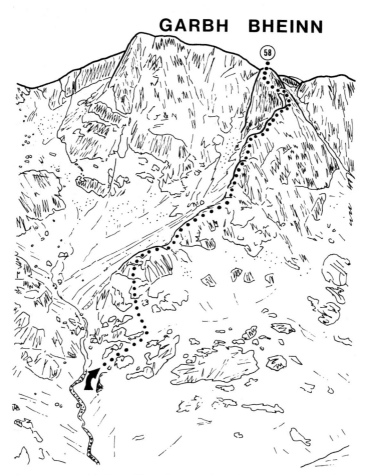

GARBH BHEINN

along vegetated ledges. There is an awkward move to reach a ledge above two blocks

Ascend a groove trending slightly left and make a difficult move to exit onto a heather ledge below a massive perched boulder. Move up to the left side of this and then climb a steep leftward trending groove on good holds to easier ground.

Continue up the ridge to a flattening, with the final rock tower visible above. Carry on along the easy ridge to a narrowing where a gully, with a steep left wall, runs down to the corrie on the left. Some distance above, the ridge develops into a delightful arête, which curves round the right-hand side of the final tower, and is separated from it by a large gully.

Stay on the arête as much as possible. One section necessitates an awkward step onto a small ledge. The final section consists of a sharp edge of rock with a grassy groove immediately right of it. Start up the groove, then step left and finish along the arête.

A grassy terrace joins the top of the arête to the flank of the rock tower. Traverse left to reach a massive slab. Get established on this and go up it to the very crest of the tower. A superb finale - not to be missed.

Follow the crest delightfully to the top. Turn left and continue to the summit of Garbh Bheinn. The best descent is to carry on over the next top (823m), and then go down the Sron a' Gharbh Choire Bhig back to the road.

* * *

There is scope for scrambling on several other parts of the mountain, notably from Bealach Feith 'n Amean at the very head of Coire an Iubhair, and on the east sides of Sron a' Gharbh Choire Mhoir and Sron a' Gharbh Choire Bhig. Mention should also be made of The Great Ridge which, by the direct start, is a classic Very Difficult rock climb. It takes a magnificent line direct to the summit of Garbh Bheinn. Details of the route can be found in 'Rock and Ice Climbs in Lochaber and Badenoch', by A.C.Stead and J.R.Marshall.

The circuit of Coire an Iubhair makes a marvellous hillwalk. It is best done anti-clockwise, in which case the following scramble can be easily included by a short detour, after descending from Sgorr Mhic Eacharna.

59. EAST FACE OF BEINN BHEAG   Grade 1   **

It would be possible to approach this route from Glen Gour, but it is more pleasing to descend to it from Bealach nan Aingidh during a round of Coire an Iubhair, *(corrie of the yew-tree)*. Most of the route is on beautiful slabs.

Descend northwards from the bealach, and cross two minor streams to reach the first low tongue of rock just above the 400m contour. A sheep track traverses below it.

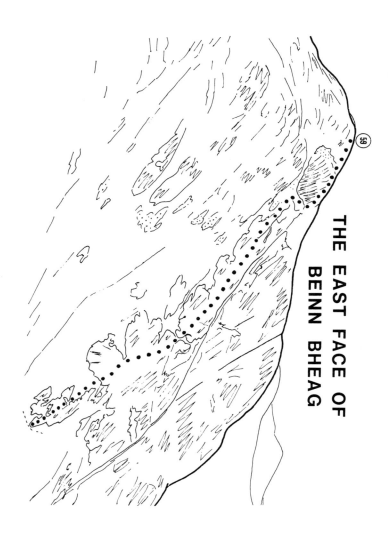

THE EAST FACE OF BEINN BHEAG

59

Go up easily to the next piece of slabby rock immediately above. Climb this to the right of some narrow wet streaks. Continue on grass to a short, but rather steeper rock step. Find a way up just left of a tiny tree on good holds.

Ascend more easily up a series of rock slabs trending slightly right. Eventually reach a particularly prominent slab, and go up this near a conspicuous smooth plane of rock. Continue more easily to the steep headwall some distance above.

The middle section can only be ascended by rock climbing, and to the left is too easy, so move up to the right-hand end. Go up a short distance and find a line trending leftwards up more vegetated ground. The scrambling finishes about 200m from the summit of Beinn Bheag *(small mountain)*.

Continue over the summit, and descend to the lochan perched on the Bealach Feith 'n Amean. From here seek out any amount of scrambling on the Sron Lag nan Gamhna leading to the top of what is known as North-East Buttress, on the north side of Garbh Bheinn. Continue past the top of Pinnacle Ridge to the summit of Garbh Bheinn, and so continue the circuit.

*   *   *

The other main area for scrambling in Ardgour is on the hills south of Glenfinnan, overlooking Loch Shiel. The principal mountain is Sgurr Ghiubhsachain, but the best rock outcrops occur on the western flanks of Sgorr nan Cearc and Meall Doire na Mnatha, which both lie on the east side of Coire Ghiubhsachain. Some rock climbing has been done here.

The hills are approached by turning south off the Mallaig road some 2km before Glenfinnan. Park near a locked gate at a bridge over the Callop River, (G.R. 924 792). Go over the bridge, turn right and follow a track which after 2km runs alongside Loch Shiel.

A good circuit can be made round Coire Ghiubhsachain by starting up the north-west ridge of Sgorr nan Cearc. A large buttress at a height of 400m gives some reasonable scrambling. However, the outing now described is on the most northern hill of the group, and is slightly more accessible. It gives very fine views despite its modest height, and is ideal for a short day or just an evening.

MEALL NA H-AIRIGH

The route traverses Meall na h-Airigh *(hill of the Prince)* from west

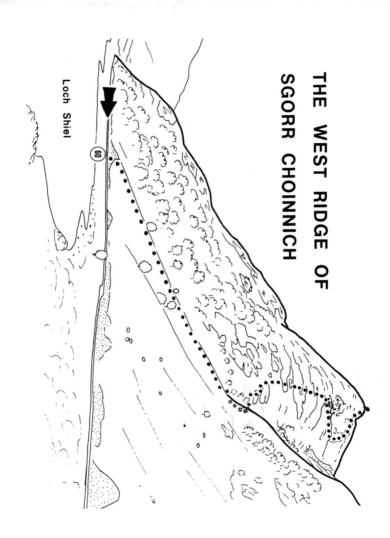

THE WEST RIDGE OF
SGORR CHOINNICH

Loch Shiel

60

to east. The scrambling is all on the west ridge of Sgorr Choinnich, a barely discernible top some 300m west of the summit. The best part of the route is the top section.

60. THE WEST RIDGE OF SGORR CHOINNICH

Grade 2 *

Walk along Loch Shiel for just over 1km to where a long gully curves leftwards up the hillside. Leave the track at some bouldery debris near a small stream from the gully, (G.R. 895 790). Go up the right bank of the stream for some distance to a rock wall. Traverse left into the gully and walk up it until directly below a conspicuous slab of white rock high on the right wall.

Traverse up and left along a sheep track out of the gully onto the broad ridge on the left. This is very heathery, but interspersed with delightful sections of gneiss and pegmatite slab. Climb the first short section of rock, but avoid the second on the left. Continue for some distance hunting out any further sections of slab. Reach flatter ground with huge boulders below a much steeper rock buttress.

This is too difficult and unpleasant at the front, so traverse some distance round to the right, and ascend a prominent rock ridge. Continue in the same line, then move left slightly and gain a rightward curving ridge from the left. Go up the ridge, then traverse right. Move back left to finish steeply on good holds just by the summit. Continue easily to the summit of Meall na h-Airigh.

There are magnificent views of Loch Shiel, Glenfinnan and surrounding hills, as well as distant views of Loch Eil and Ben Nevis. A rapid descent can be made of the broad east ridge. Head left near the bottom, and follow the edge of a plantation back to the bridge over the Callop River.

*   *   *

The Forcan Ridge (Route 69)

THE NORTHERN
GROUP

The hills of the northern group are dissected by several major glens and lochs, which all run in an east-west direction. Two sea-lochs, Loch Nevis and Loch Hourne, cut into the coastline and embrace the district of Knoydart. There is no through road around the coast, and the only roads to penetrate the interior of the area are the long single-track roads which finish at the head of Loch Arkaig and Kinloch Hourn. Such inaccessibility helps to keep this as one of the wildest and loneliest parts of the country. There is only one drawback - it is also the wettest.

On the north side of the Mallaig road there are some very pleasant hills. Streap for example gives a fine ridge walk. There are also innumerable small rock outcrops in the Morar district north of Lochailort. Some scrambling can be had, for example on Druim Fiaclach overlooking Loch nan Uamh, but it does not amount to much.

* * *

The Loch Lochy Hills

The first two scrambles included here are at the eastern end of
the area on the hills overlooking Loch Lochy. They can both be seen
from the opposite side of the loch on the A82 near the Letterfinlay
Lodge Hotel. They are approached along forest tracks starting from
Clunes or Kilfinnan.

*　*　*

MEALL DUBH

Meall Dubh lies equidistant from Clunes and Kilfinnan, and directly
across from the Letterfinlay Lodge Hotel. Its south-east face is split
by deep gullies and guarded at the base by a deep ravine. The best
approach entails a walk of 5km along the upper forest track from
Clunes.

61. CENTRAL BUTTRESS, SOUTH-EAST FACE
Grade 3　*

Park at Clunes and soon after take the left fork in the forest track.
Walk north-east for 5km until the track ends at a point overlooking
the Dearg Allt *(red stream)*. In one or two places before this, the
track has been blocked or washed away by streams in flood.

The problem now is to identify the bottom of a ride which gives
access to the hillside below the scramble. Walk back along the track
and very shortly reach a bend. Go about 80m past the bend and the
ride can then be found on the right. Unfortunately the bottom of it is
difficult to make out, but it becomes much more distinct as height is
gained. A short distance up, it is possible to look directly across Loch
Lochy to the Letterfinlay Lodge Hotel.

Emerge on the open hillside and head straight up to a prominent
tree overlooking the ravine of the Dearg Allt. The scramble ascends
the buttress directly across from here, but a somewhat circuitous
route has to be taken to avoid the ravine and the uninviting lower
part of the face. The advantage of this approach is that a good view
can be had of the traverse to the buttress.

Go left up the ridge overlooking the ravine, to a tiny col which is
also the source of a small stream flowing down to the forest on the
left, (G.R. 233 926). Now follow a sheep track across the upper part
of the Dearg Allt, and make a slightly descending traverse right to

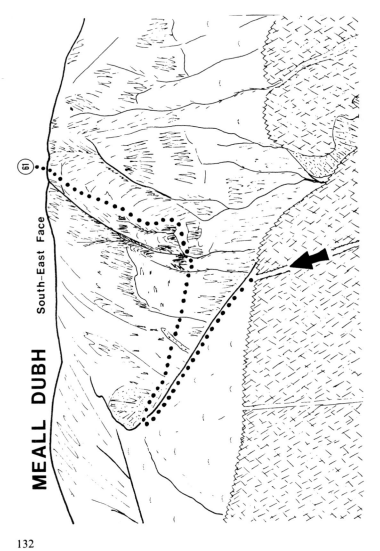

MEALL DUBH

South-East Face

61

gain the buttress. No difficulties should be encountered if the sheep track is followed throughout, and the stream on the left side of the buttress can then be crossed easily too.

Once on the buttress, head up in a rightwards direction to a small but conspicuous conifer. The terrain is steep and heathery, and this is the hardest and least pleasant part of the outing. Go right to a slabby section of rock overlooking the stream on the right. Either struggle round it on the right or climb up it (harder), then move back leftwards to the centre of the buttress.

The main difficulties are now over and the remainder of the buttress is more enjoyable. Continue up easier angled ground and ascend some small rock outcrops. There are no difficulties which cannot be avoided, but most fun can be had by keeping as direct a line as possible.

Move slightly left at one point to ascend a small recess. Higher up another outcrop with a slabby right wall can also be climbed. The buttress then levels out before steepening slightly again near the finish. Arrive at a small top on the east ridge of Meall Dubh. This is a marvellous viewpoint for the Great Glen and a host of different hills.

A beautiful circuit can be made by traversing over the summit of Meall Dubh, and then continuing round over Meall na Teanga and Meall Coire Lochain. From the summit of the latter continue round the rim of Coire Lochain and start descending the Sron Bhreac which points in the direction of the Letterfinlay Lodge Hotel. At a height of 600m turn left and head north-north-west down an easy ramp to a lovely lochan. Then turn right and make for the top of a large ride (G.R. 227 912) which leads down to the forest track used in the approach.

*   *   *

SEAN MHEALL

The next scramble is best approached from Kilfinnan. Either turn off for Kilfinnan near the southern end of Loch Oich, or park at Laggan Locks, cross over the Caledonian Canal and then walk 1km to Kilfinnan. Continue along a rough track, pass some chalets and after a further 2½km reach the start of a path which goes up the north bank of the Allt Glas-Dhoire. Recent tree-felling has cleared this part of the forest. The path passes beneath the south face of Sean Mheall *(old hill)*, to the Cam Bhealach *(crooked pass)* between Meall Dubh and Sron a' Choire Ghairbh.

62. SOUTH FACE OF SEAN MHEALL   Grade 2   *

The scramble is in three parts. It starts by ascending the bed of a gully, then it goes up the vegetated hillside on the right, and it finishes up a wedge-shaped buttress between two forks of the gully.

Follow the path for 750m to where the stream from the forked gully crosses it, (G.R. 244 937). This is about 300m past the boundary fence of the forest. Go up the stream-bed on boulders at first. Then negotiate a series of short waterfalls. If the water is too high or the rock too daunting it is easy to divert onto either bank. After climbing the left side of a largish waterfall, the streamway becomes broken and unpleasant, so exit up the right (east) bank just before a slope of debris, with a much larger waterfall in view.

Follow steep heather on the right bank for quite some distance. This is rather tedious. Pass a fork in the stream. Keep on the right bank, then shortly after passing two small trees on the opposite bank, follow a sheep track which leads left across the stream onto the heathery buttress.

Try to maintain a central line where possible. Ascend a small broken rock rib. More heather follows. The buttress then becomes more rocky and interesting, although most difficulties can be avoided if required. Go up between two huge boulders. The angle eases slightly, then the buttress narrows. Arrive at a rock nose. Move round to the right and climb back left onto the crest. Continue more easily to the summit.

A pleasant walk of 2km leads over some minor tops to the summit of Sron a' Choire Ghairbh. Return to the col at 878m and pick up a path which zig-zags down to a lower bealach. Turn left and after 2km pass the start of the scramble.

*   *   *

Knoydart

The wildest, wettest and most wonderful area in this guide is called Knoydart. Its scrambling interest can only be of secondary importance to the wilderness experience it has to offer. It is not the easiest of places to do justice to in a weekend, and its special qualities are best savoured by backpacking over several days.

The two most common approaches are from the head of Loch Arkaig and from Kinloch Hourn. Boats can also be chartered along Loch Nevis and across Barrisdale Bay. From Kinloch Hourn an undulating track goes along the south shore of Loch Hourn to Barrisdale, where camping is permitted and bothy accommodation is available at G.R. 871 042. From Strathan at the head of Loch Arkaig, a forestry track on the south side of the River Dessarry goes west past A' Chuil bothy. Where the track ends a path can be picked up on the north side of the river which leads over Bealach an Lagain Duibh, past Lochan a' Mhaim to the head of Loch Nevis. Sourlies bothy is situated at G.R. 868 950, but it can be very crowded at certain times in the spring and early summer, and it is not always wise to bank on finding room there. Even wilderness areas are getting popular these days.

*   *   *

BEN ADEN

Not far from the western end of Loch Quoich there is a rugged little mountain called Ben Aden. It is within reasonable distance of Sourlies, and there are good views of it from the lower reaches of the River Carnach. It can also be reached from Barrisdale via Gleann Unndalain.

63. THE SOUTH FACE OF BEN ADEN   Grade 2

This route is best approached from the Loch Nevis side. If coming from Sourlies, walk along the shore for ¼km (not at high tide), and make for a footbridge over the River Carnach at G.R. 865 964. Follow a faint path on the north bank, until it is possible to recross the river in the vicinity of G.R. 885 975. Head east beside the Allt Achadh a' Ghlinne to where a wire fence slants across the stream, (G.R. 897 978).

Move up the hillside on the north side of the stream and slant up right to gain a broad ridge shortly after an initial steep section.

Ben Aden and Sgurr Na Ciche from the River Carnach (Route 63)

Follow a series of grassy and lichenous rock ribs. Cross a small col on the ridge. Continue in the same line taking in short rock sections from time to time.

At a second, less distinctive col head across right to a slabby wall with a prominent white vein in it. Ascend this by moving first left, then right. The larger grey slab above is too difficult, so creep round it on the left. Continue up rightward trending easy slabs. Huge boulders lie in a faint gully on the left.

Go up grass to another rock band, and zig-zag up this some distance right of a weeping wall. The rock is excellent. Continue easily up slabs and grass to a terrace below the east ridge of the mountain. There are fine views of Loch Quoich from here.

Go easily up to the east ridge and follow it to the summit. There are splendid views of Sgurr na Ciche and Loch Nevis, as well as Luinne Bheinn, Loch Hourn, and even Rhum and Eigg. The best way back from here is to go around the head of the Allt Achadh a' Ghlinne, over Meall a' Choire Dhuibh and on to Sgurr na Ciche. Then descend the long south-west ridge, the Druim a' Ghoirtein, to Sourlies.

64. THE EAST-NORTH-EAST RIDGE OF BEN ADEN

Grade 1   **

This long scenic ridge is not so easy to approach now as it was before the damming of Loch Quoich. Possibly the best approach is from Barrisdale up Gleann Unndalain, followed by a long descent to the eastern end of the beautiful Lochan nam Breac *(lochan of the trout)*. Another route is to follow the River Carnach from Loch Nevis, or to ascend the Allt Achadh a' Ghlinne, and cross the Bealach a' Choire Chruaidh.

There are some poor stepping-stones where the Allt Lochan na Cruadhach flows into the eastern end of Lochan nam Breac. From here follow the path towards Loch Quoich for about 250m, then head right up a prominent grassy bay, with a large slanting rock band above on the left. Move right to gain a ridge overlooking Lochan nam Breac. Continue for some distance, and cross two boggy cols. Eventually gain a better defined ridge at G.R. 914 989.

From here the ridge leads west for 700m. Weave to and fro on magnificent rough slabs. These give some of the best scrambling on the route. The ridge then curves round to the left, and at a height of 750m there is a huge platform of bare rock.

Move slightly left, then back right and follow a much narrower ridge for some distance. Go over a small tower and continue easily to the summit. The north face of the mountain looks impressive from the ridge. The south-west flank of the mountain gives the best descent to the River Carnach. There is a path down the east side of Meall a' Choire Dhuibh, which leads round to the western end of Loch Quoich.

*   *   *

A beautiful circular walk can be done from Barrisdale, which is even worthwhile when all the hills are in cloud. Go up Gleann Unndalain, and descend to the eastern end of Lochan nam Breac. Continue over a small col to the western end of Loch Quoich. Go along the north side of this arm of the loch, and then turn off left into Gleann Cosaidh. Cross the Abhainn Chosaidh. This can be a problem after heavy rain. Go round the north side of Loch an Lagain Aintheich and descend Glen Barrisdale. Most of the route is on well constructed path, and yet it still has a wonderfully untamed feel about it. Such is the magic of Knoydart. Only the dam on Loch Quoich spoils things.

The next scramble is convenient for those staying in Barrisdale. It can be included as part of a high level route back to the Kinloch Hourn road.

65. THE SOUTH FACE OF AN CAISTEAL   Grade 3   **

Follow the path up Glen Barrisdale for nearly 3km to a grassy **embayment where a small stream flows south-east across the** southern flank of An Caisteal *(the castle)*. Carry on a short distance to a small rock slab, which is right by the path, (G.R. 898 035).

Climb the slab and continue more easily above. By weaving to and fro it is possible to stay on rock for much of the way. Avoid a wall with a prominent quartz vein by moving left. Reach the top of a knoll and descend slightly to a col. Skirt round the obvious rock band on the left, then follow an easy grassy gully back right. Head left to a large open terrace.

The hillside above has many outcrops of slabby rock, with some steeper rocks walls. Move up to the first small rock band. Clamber over boulders just left of a solitary tree, and scramble up the rock above.

Move up, then make a long rising traverse to the left on an obvious broad, bouldery ramp, so as to avoid the next, larger rock band. In places, the left edge of the ramp can be climbed on rough rock slabs. Follow the ramp until it ends and then walk right along the first narrow terrace. Alternatively, just before the ramp ends, move across to the rock band on the right. Make a short traverse right along a ledge with boulders, then go delicately up, trending left, on slabby rock stained brown by lichen.

Ascend some easy rock slabs trending right, until a larger wall is reached. Move up to this and pass it by grass and boulders on the left. (Climbers will be able to find a delightful route across and up the wall.) Follow another slabby buttress above.

Go up slightly boggy ground to the next large rock band. Ascend this at an obvious break left of centre. There are some interesting problems for climbers on the left. Near the top of the break a grassy terrace leads right. Head up to a short rock slab, and continue to a major rock band above and right.

Go up to the left-most section of wall, just right of a wet grassy area. Scramble up a fine staircase with some large step-ups. Now traverse a long way right, across a slab to the furthest grassy corner on the right. Scramble up this and continue up a slabby wall and groove trending right. Move back left up a heathery slope, or ascend

138

the difficult slab on the left. Gain a rightward sloping slabby corner and move up until it is possible to scramble up the slab on the right to easier ground.

Go across to a short, broken buttress and find a way up trending right. Continue to a broad terrace. Head rightwards up the grassy hillside to the next section of rock slabs. Scramble up grassy ledges trending right. Pass to the left of a huge boulder and keep moving up right on slabby rocks to an easier angled bouldery slope.

Head up right to the final section of slabby rocks. Go diagonally right, past the first mass of rock to a much larger outcrop. Start in the centre and scramble up trending right to a narrow grass ledge. Follow this right to a prominent vein of white and pink pegmatite. There are several options from here. The hardest line follows the pegmatite vein up left, passing a huge boulder at half way. This is sustained and deserves a 3(S) grade. Another line starts further right **at an easy grassy groove. It crosses heather to reach a slabby wall and then follows further heather and vegetation up left. All this can be** avoided by moving even further right and ascending easy grooves and ribs.

A variety of lines can be followed on the upper section. String together any number of small slabby outcrops and finish suddenly on the east ridge. The summit is about 400m away. There is no well defined top, only a jumble of small rock outcrops, boulders, hollows and lochans. The views are magnificent. Some rock climbs have been done on the opposite side of the mountain.

A straightforward descent can be made by going back along the east ridge to a bealach between An Caisteal and Meall nan Eun at G.R. 901 045. A gully on the right leads down to a stream which joins the River Barrisdale near a waterfall and large pool. Those returning to the Kinloch Hourn road can continue over Meall nan Eun *(hill of the birds)*. and Sgurr nan Eugallt, before descending the north-east ridge of the latter to a stalker's path which starts at a height of 550m. The path is not very easy to follow in places, but it takes a delightful route down to reach the road at the ruin of Coireshubh near Loch Coire Shubh.

LADHAR BHEINN

Ladhar Bheinn *(forked mountain)* is one of the finest and most secluded mountains in the area. The circuit of Coire Dhorrcail makes a very memorable outing and it can be started by either of the scrambles now described. The normal approach is from Barrisdale along a path which heads north-west from a bridge over the River Barrisdale at G.R. 871 041. Cross a stream and head south-west. The path is difficult to follow for a short section, but then it heads back north-west again by a series of short zig-zags. Continue north-west, then lose height slightly and turn left into the mouth of Coire Dhorrcail - a dramatic sight.

66. THE NORTH-EAST RIDGE OF
STOB A' CHEARCAILL   Grade 1   *

Just before reaching the high point on the path round to the mouth of Coire Dhorrcail, head up left to a fine viewpoint at the foot of a broad ridge called Creag Bheithe. Follow the ridge for nearly 2km to a col below the steep nose of Stob a' Chearcaill *(peak of the circle or hoop)*.

Zig-zag up the nose on narrow grassy ledges, with large thin flakes of schistose rock. It is steep for about 30m and then it eases slightly. There are some awkward steps, but most difficulties can be avoided. It then steepens again, before easing gradually to the summit. The route is very much trickier in descent.

Continue along the undulating ridge for more than 600m to an un-named top marked by a height of 849m. A very long ridge leads west-south-west from here to Inverie, the only settlement in Knoydart. Some 800m along the ridge is the aptly named Aonach Sgoilte *(split height or ridge)*. This consists of two parallel ridges, the southern one being marked by a height of 758m. An amusing little scramble can be had on the bottom section of the right-hand (northern) ridge. It is reached by a short rightwards descent from a col at the start of the southern ridge.

The normal circuit of Coire Dhorrcail is made by heading north-west from point 849m, to the Bealach Coire Dhorrcail. This gives an easy descent to Coire Dhorrcail if required. Otherwise continue along the bumpy, rocky ridge which runs along the impressive headwall of the corrie, to the summit of Ladhar Bheinn. The summit itself is a short distance along an almost level ridge running west-north-west. The trig point is about 300m past the summit on a slightly lower excrescence.

Return from the summit and descend the north-east ridge, the Ceum na Leth-coise *(step of the foot)*. This is quite steep and narrow. Go up and over the Stob Choire Odhair and then continue descending in a north-easterly direction. Eventually slant down the slope on the right, and head east to pick up the start of the stalker's path back to Barrisdale.

LADHAR BHEINN

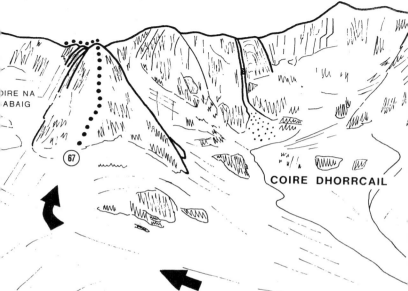

DIRE NA
ABAIG

(67)

COIRE DHORRCAIL

67. THE NORTH-EAST RIDGE OF
STOB DHORRCAIL Grade 2

This route ascends a prominent spur called Stob Dhorrcail, which juts out into Coire Dhorrcail and divides off the smaller Coire na Cabaig. It will appeal to those who specialise in scrambling on steep grass.

Follow the path from Barrisdale round into Coire Dhorrcail, and then go up the right (west) bank of the Allt Taarsuinn towards Coire na Cabaig. Swing across to the right and gain the front nose of the Stob from the left. The first section of the route is the hardest. As the angle eases it becomes more pleasant. There are fine views of the magnificent north-west face of Stob a' Chearcaill.

From the top of the Stob continue along a very enjoyable section of ridge, over several small tops. Traverse slightly right to join the normal circuit of Coire Dhorrcail just before Bealach Coire Dhorrcail. Continue as for the previous route.

141

South Glen Shiel

Some very fine hills border the A87 road through Glen Shiel to Kyle of Lochalsh. On the north side are the Five Sisters of Kintail, and on the south side are the Cluanie Ridge and The Saddle. Both sides of the glen make superb long traverses, normally done from east to west. The Cluanie Ridge has seven Munroes in its 14km length, and only between the last two tops does it drop much below 800m.

The first scramble samples part of the Cluanie Ridge including the highest top, Aonach air Chrith. It makes a very pleasant outing for those not feeling up to the full traverse, and since it starts and finishes in the same place, only one means of transport is required.

68. THE NORTH RIDGE OF AONACH AIR CHRITH
Grade 1   *

Start from a parking bay on the north side of the A87 at G.R. 043 114, opposite the Allt Coire a' Chuil Droma Bhig. A stalker's path starts from the south side of the road and then divides in two, one branch going up the Druim Thollaidh and the other up the Druim Coire nan Eirecheanach. The outing now described makes a circuit of Coire nan Eirecheanach.

Leave the road near a 'beware falling rocks' sign, and follow the stalker's path until across the Allt Coire a' Chuil Droma Bhig. Then head roughly south-east for almost 2km to a rock buttress at the northern end of A'Chioch, the north-east top of Aonach air Chrith. Cross the Allt Coire nan Eirecheanach about halfway.

Reach the first tongue of slabby rock at a height of about 400m, and move onto it from the right. Ascend same and then pick a way up a succession of minor rock steps, until a larger mass of rock is reached.

Move up the left side of a prominent groove, bounded by a rock wall on the right. When progress is barred by a steeper section, traverse right onto a large rock slab. Continue traversing right, below a rock wall, until able to find a way up at the far right-hand end. Go up more easily via one minor rock band to a more open and grassy section of hillside.

Make for an obvious crag some distance above. Move round to the right of it, then follow an easy line back left to surmount it. Continue pleasantly to the top of A' Chioch - a flat grassy summit.

Descend to a faint col, then go rightwards slightly up grassy terrain, thereby avoiding the worst of the scree. Join the crest of the Druim na Ciche, which is the north ridge of Aonach air Chrith, and follow this easily for some distance.

The ridge then starts to become more rocky, and the best fun is to be had by balancing along the very crest. Descend slightly from a small top, and then negotiate some narrow flakes of rock. Go along a narrow section of horizontal ridge, and make a short ascent on grass to the summit.

Aonach air Chrith means 'trembling ridge', but all the trembling should now be over. Turn right and follow the ridge easily for 2km over Maol Chinn-dearg *(bold red top)*. This is the best section of the Cluanie Ridge. It is quite narrow, but never difficult, and there are fine views.

From the 981m summit turn right and descend the Druim Coire nan Eirecheanach. Pick up the stalker's path which leads back to the starting point.

*   *   *

The last two scrambles are at the western end of Glen Shiel on two Munroes called The Saddle and Sgurr na Sgine. *(peak of the knife)*. They are easily combined in one outing by doing a figure of eight, as described below.

69. THE FORCHAN RIDGE   Grade 1 or 2   ***

The east ridge of Sgurr na Forchan *(the forked peak)* is one of the most delightful scrambles in this guide. A good stalker's path which rises to almost 500m makes the approach to it relatively effortless. The continuation of the ridge to the summit of The Saddle is also very good. Combined with an ascent of Sgurr na Sgine, it makes a thoroughly enjoyable outing.

Leave the A87 about 350m north-west of the Malagan Bridge at G.R. 968 142. Follow the path for about 2km to where it finishes at Bealach na Craoibhe. Turn left and ascend Meall Odhar, then head south-west for about 500m to the start of the ridge. There are very few route-finding problems from here on. Several small slabby outcrops can be climbed on the first part of the ridge, but the more interesting upper section starts after a rightwards deflection of the ridge at a height of 800m.

Go over a small top to reach the beginning of the narrow section. This is never as difficult as it looks from a distance. The Grade 2 line stays right on the crest the whole way, whereas the Grade 1 line takes

The Forcan Ridge (Route 69)

all the easy options just off the crest. One or two blocks on the crest give interesting problems, but for much of the way it is a matter of balancing along knife-edges of rock. There is a superb horizontal knife-edge just off the ridge on the left at one point. Those with a head for heights may enjoy making a short detour along it. It is very photogenic.

The descent from the summit of Sgurr na Forchan is the most difficult part of the route if it is made directly to a gap, but easier (Grade 1) options are also available. Continue along the narrow ridge, over a small top to the summit of The Saddle at 1010m. The trig point sits on another small peak of equal height about 150m further on. There are two lochans just below this second top, which are welcome sights in hot weather.

Descend south-east past the lochans, then slant across the south flank of The Saddle to Bealach Coire Mhalagain. Climb up to join the ridge between Faochag and Sgurr na Sgine at a top of 879m. Turn right for Sgurr na Sgine, but instead of ascending its north ridge follow an obvious terrace which curves left across the north-east face of the mountain.

70. NORTH-EAST RIDGE OF SGURR NA SGINE

Grade 1   *

This scramble can be approached up Coire Toiteil, but the terrace mentioned above gives access to it by a descending traverse from the north.

At the lowest part of the ridge there is a rightward slanting rock band with large boulders at its base. Move round to the left of this, and follow the right-hand of two parallel slabby rock ribs, which are separated by a grassy groove. Try to keep position on the rib as the exposure on the right becomes more noticeable. When the rib peters out, break up through to more vegetated ground above.

Continue some distance until rock steps develop again. Follow the twisting ridge and as it becomes sharper try to maintain position on the crest. There are several short rock sections, before the angle eases and the summit cairn is reached. The south-east face falls abruptly from the summit.

Head north-west to a top which is only 1m lower than the main summit. Then descend the north ridge and continue round to the summit of Faochag *(the whelk)*. Return to the road by descending the north-east ridge. It is unremittingly steep.

*   *   *

APPENDIX I

BIBLIOGRAPHY

Climbing Guides

Lochaber and Badenóch by C.Stead and J.R.Marshall, 1981, Scottish Mountaineering Club.

Glencoe and Glen Etive by K.Crocket, 1980, Scottish Mountaineering Trust.

Ben Nevis by J.R.Marshall, Revised 1979, Scottish Mountaineering Club.

Scottish Climbs by H.MacInnes, 1981, Constable.

Glen Nevis and the Lochaber Outcrops by E.Grindley, 1985, Cicerone Press.

General Mountaineering/Walking Books

The Western Highlands by D.Bennet, 1983, Scottish Mountaineering Club.

The Central Highlands by P.Hodgkiss, 1984, Scottish Mountaineering Club.

Scottish Mountain Climbs by D.Bennet, 1979, Batsford.

The Big Walks compiled by K.Wilson and R.Gilbert, 1980, Diadem.

Classic Walks compiled by K.Wilson and R.Gilbert, 1982, Diadem.

Hamish's Mountain Walk by H.Brown, 1978, Victor Gollancz/1980, Granada.

Mountaineering in Scotland/Undiscovered Scotland by W.H.Murray, 1982, Diadem.

Mountaincraft and Leadership by E.Langmuir, 1984, Scottish Sports Council & the Mountainwalking Leader Training Board.

Gaelic Place Names

Place Names of Lochaber by L.MacKinnon, 1973, Saltire Society (Lochaber Branch).

Understand Highland Place-Names compiled and published by W.Owen of Invermoriston.

Place Names on Maps of Scotland and Wales, 1973, published by the Ordnance Survey.

Dwelly's Illustrated Gaelic to English Dictionary, Ninth Edition 1977, Gairm.

Geology Reference Books

Geology of Scotland edited by G.Y.Craig, 1983, Scottish Academic Press.

The Geology of Ben Nevis and Glen Coe - Memoir of the Geological Survey of Great Britain, 1976, HMSO.

Grampian Highlands (Regional Geology of Great Britain Handbook), 1966, HMSO.

Northern Highlands (Regional Geology of Great Britain Handbook), 1960, HMSO.

Minerals, Rocks and Fossils by W.R.Hamilton, A.R.Woolley & A.C.Bishop, 1974, Hamlyn.

Encyclopaedia of Rocks and Minerals, 1983, MacDonald & Co.

Geology and Scenery in Scotland by J.B.Whittow, 1979, Penguin.

Other Reference Books

The Scottish Highlands by W.H.Murray, 1976, Scottish Mountaineering Trust.

The Making of the Highlands by M.Brander, 1980, Constable.

Thomas Telford by R.M.Pearce, 1978, Shire Publications Ltd.

The Highlands and Islands by F.Fraser Darling & J.Morton Boyd, 1964, Collins.

The Drove Roads of Scotland by A.R.B. Haldane, 1968, Edinburgh University Press.

*   *   *

APPENDIX II

A GLOSSARY OF GAELIC WORDS FOR HILL-GOERS

Gaelic words had different spellings and different meanings in different parts of the Highlands. Over the years names have been corrupted or Anglicised, and their meanings are now obscure. Despite all this, some familiarity with Gaelic can add interest to an outing on the hills. Specific names are explained in places in the text, and only more general terms are listed below.

abar, (aber), obair	confluence of a river, marshy ground
abhainn	stream, river
allt	mountain stream
alltan	small mountain stream
aonach	steep hill, height, ridge
bàn	white
beag	small
bealach	pass, col
beinn, (ben)	hill, mountain
beinnean	little hill
binnein, binnean	pinnacle, high conical hill
bidein, bidean	pointed, sharp-topped
bidean, bidean	peak, pinnacle, summit
bodach	old man
buachaill	herdsman, shepherd
buidhe	yellow, golden
cailleach	old woman
caisteal	castle, tower
càrn, cairn	cairn, pile of stones, stony summit
cioch, ciche	breast
ciste	chest, coffin
cnap	hillock
cnoc	knoll, hillock
coire	cauldron, kettle
coire	corrie
cnàimh	bone
creag	crag, cliff
cruach	bold rounded hill
cruachan	conical hill or mountain-top
cumhang	narrow, gorge
dearg	red
druim	long back, ridge
dubh	black

eag, eige	notch, gap
eagach	notched, indented
eas	waterfall, cascade
easan	little waterfall
fada	long
fiacaill	tooth
fiaclach	toothed, jagged
fireach	hill, moor, mountain
garbh	rough, rugged
geàrr, gear	short
glas	grey, pale
gleann	valley, glen
lairig	valley or pass between mountains
loch	arm of the sea, lake
lochan	small lake
màm	large round hill
maol	bare round hill
meall	shapeless hill, mound
monadh	moor, heath, plateau
mòr	big, large, great
muileann	mill
oìd	steep rounded mountain
sgolt	split, cleft
sgòr, sgùrr	sharp hill, pointed peak
sìthean	little hill, knoll
sloc, slochd	hollow, gully, ditch
srath	plain beside a river, strath
sròn	nose, promontory, ridge
stac	high cliff, steep rock
steall	cataract, waterfall, torrent
stob	spike, stake, (pointed peak)
stuc	peak, small hill projecting from a larger one
suidhe	seat, terrace on hillside
tom	round hillock
tórr	mound, lofty hill
tulach	knoll, hillock
uaimh, uamha	cave
uisge	water, rain

INDEX TO SCRAMBLES

PRINTED BY CARNMOR PRINT & DESIGN
LONDON ROAD, PRESTON, LANCASHIRE.